CHRIST RENEWED
EVERYTHING ABOUT ME

CHRIST RENEWED EVERYTHING ABOUT ME

My journey to finally healing the inner me.

ELMINA MORISSETTE

Contents

Acknowledgments — vii
My Ministry Told In Parables — ix
Dedication — xiii

INTRODUCTION: MY JOURNEY TO TRANSFORMATION — 1

KINGDOM ENTREPRENEUR TESTIMONY — 8

1. PLANTED SEEDS OF THE ENEMY — 10
2. OVERCOMING SIN PATTERNS & GENERATIONAL CURSES — 24
3. THE POWER OF COMMUNITY — 34
4. THE POWER OF FORGIVENESS — 45
5. SIN, GOD'S GRACE & OUR BIRTHRIGHT — 59
6. WE ARE IMAGE BEARERS & OVERCOMERS — 65
7. SOCIETY'S DEPICTION OF GOD — 70
8. GOD, THROUGH THE EYES OF THE BEHOLDER — 74
9. THE DIVINE UNION — 85
10. LOVE CONQUERS ALL — 98
11. BLAME BAD DOCTRINE, NOT GOD. — 104
12. GOD'S HEALING POWER — 109

All scripture quotations, unless otherwise indicated, are taken from the Holy Bible, New International Version (NIV). Copyright © 1973, 1978, 1984, 2011 by Biblica, Inc.

Copyright © 2020 by ELMINA MORISSETTE

All rights reserved. No part of this book may be reproduced in any manner whatsoever without written permission except in the case of brief quotations embodied in critical articles and reviews.

First Printing, 2020

To learn more about Elmina Morissette, visit www.thebaemovement.com

Acknowledgments

The below-listed individuals or organizations have poured so much into my understanding of God, Purpose, Identity, and God's love. I am appreciative of how God surrounded me with great friends and outstanding literature. I will be referencing a variety of their teachings because God used them to reach me in my season of singleness. I am grateful for all their teachings during the pivotal points in my life. I am thankful for God's everlasting grace and favor. All the pressing was for a greater purpose, and I cannot wait to share my journey with you. I would have never thought God would go to such great lengths to build a relationship with me and restore me to him. He helped me to understand his words and know that he loves me. Neither death nor life can indeed separate us from God's love. Knowledge is only power if you activate it, and so I did. All we must do is show up to receive the blessings God has for us. Understanding that he wants to increase his children. He already laid out the provisions, the people you need to help you, and all you will need to fulfill your calling. You just need to show up and let him show out. The harvest is plenty, but the laborers are few. We need to renew our minds and understand that God is for us and nothing can be against us. God talks highly of us in the bible, and throughout the text, you will see how we are all fearfully and wonderfully made in God's image. Everybody has their unique path/walk with God. God hears you. Come to him with a sincere heart, and he will guide you. You cannot impact those you choose to insult. The only enemy in this world is the devil. Let me prove it to you.

Transformation Church, Tulsa OK
Change Church, Pastor Dharius Daniels
Elevation Church, Steven Furtick

Real Life Church, Clermont, FL
Reach Ministries, Orlando, FL
Serenity Tabernacle International Ministries, Reverend Ruby
Soul Care by Dr. Rob Reimer
Carla R Cannon of Carla R Cannon Enterprises
Redefined Church, Jerry Flowers

My Ministry told in Parables

This book was written for believers, non-believers, and agnostic believers. My purpose here today is not to force anyone to change. It is to give my testimony and understanding of the Lord through various literature and teachings of his word and intimate conversations with God. Revelation cannot be forced on anyone. Revelation is a choice; when someone is ready to receive, they will, and when someone is not ready to receive, they may not. I do pray through this book that God softens your heart to incline your mind to my teachings as I plant a seed of understanding. I cannot do what the Holy Spirit does, which is provide revelation to the soul. My only purpose is to give my testimony and use the word of God to help curate understanding and provoke thought. An individual can take this information before God and seek guidance from him, and he will reveal it to you. Go to God with a sincere heart. Meditate on his word because religious practices are not the goal. It is a relationship with God that is the goal of Christianity. When we move from relationship to repetition of cultural practices, we lose sight of God and only gain religion and not spirituality.

God will use the Holy Spirit through me to provide a breakthrough to others, and I am just a sounding board of information of his word and testimony. Never allow the lack of your exposure to make you doubt the existence of a thing. You must be able to listen if you want to evolve. You cannot change without provision and challenge. Let me be clear, I do not want you to read what I am not writing, and I do not want you to misunderstand what I mean in my story. I only have good intentions and a love for God's children in all I say. I can never judge someone when I have sinned and need the grace and mercy of God. I do believe evaluated experiences are the best teachers. Remember that the enemy tries to destroy your heart as a method to distract you from purpose and destiny, so always use discernment.

I have learned over this past year that worldly things have no true value to me. I used to think that all the things that I had were important. I realized that my abandonment issues lead to me placing value in things and people and not in God. When nutritionists recommend us to eat smaller portions to train our stomach not to store unnecessary fat. The stomach would store the fat because it did not know when the next meal would be, and to avoid hunger, it made a reserve of fat. In this way, I held onto things because I placed my security in possession and wealth instead of the power of God.

For this reason, I also held on to things and people longer than necessary and tried to control situations because I did not want to lack them ever again. Through God, I understood that I would never lack and be generous because my God is generous. He showers me with blessings that I do not deserve because he loves me. God knows what I need, and he will provide for my every need. I sometimes used to fear that he could not meet my needs because his needs were different from mine. However, he understands my current situation, and he would not tell me to trust him if he did not plan to secure me in all things. So, I stopped overthinking the next step and started to trust in him to lead me. Allowing God to lead me was a trust exercise that built my faith. It is something you must enter and pursue every day. Sometimes we may fall short because it seems a little scary, and that is completely fine because our Father knows us, and he will work it out for us in the end, regardless.

Incremental growth is still growth, and he acknowledges that. Do not sweat the small things. Be mindful that they do exist and make efforts to improve. Do not focus on everything that you got wrong but on the things that you got right. God gave us grace through Christ Jesus so that we may focus more on progression than transgression.

So, repentance is key. No longer should we allow society or the devil to condemn us after God has accepted our repentance. Changing our mindset would help us live more with a positive growth mindset rather than a negative mindset of resentment and regret. God says that when we repent, he cast our sins into the sea of forgetfulness, and so should we. The only time you should remember what you have done is to extend grace and mercy towards the next person and to praise God for his long-suffering love for us. No one is perfect, and God sent Jesus to die for us so that we no longer must keep track of all our sins. Instead, live every day with purpose and meaning and understanding that we are all in this for the glory of God and not for validation from a man.

I went from planning and coordinating everything because I thought I knew what was best for me, to leave it in God's hands. I spent my time feeling like I can control everything, but I realized that God is in control. He qualified me for all things, and he is the one that blesses me with everything I have. He secures me in any position, role, or opportunity that I obtain. All good and perfect things come from the Lord. I began to include him with my goals and visions because it is easier to get the answers to the test than it is to guess the answers and fail the test. I choose now to ask God, "what is next?" because he is the author of my story. He knows how the story ends, so why try to grab the pen and mess up this divine destiny God has in store for me. I realized that certain things that I pursued were not of God's will for me, and as hard as it was to let certain things go, I do not regret it because it made me a better person and the woman I am today. I would not have gotten there without understanding that a mindset change and reconciliation were the keys to my success. Even as I write this book, I realize more that I have gone through a lot of tests that have built my faith in the past two years. Every time I tell my testimony to someone, I notice that it helps them get the breakthrough they needed through God, so this made me write it all down. From my perspective, I was only making incremental steps to where God wanted me to be, but for others, it was a true transformation that sometimes I do not notice until someone else tells me. Every day, as I grow spiritually, I evolve more into the woman that I am destined to be, and it is exciting. It used to be a little scary for me, but now I am courageous. I know my destiny is meant for greatness, so I just need to continue to increase my boldness and just show people God's love.

Dedication

This book is dedicated to my loving family and friends. To all who've been there for me on my journey to the best version of myself in Christ. No family is perfect, and we have had our dysfunctions like all human families, but I am grateful for providing me a loving, stable and faith filled home. I am eternally grateful to God for my family and friends.

INTRODUCTION: MY JOURNEY TO TRANSFORMATION

As for many people, 2020 was a pivotal year. It brought enlightenment to my faith in God. The version of myself that I needed to become I would not have noticed without being in my singleness season. I needed to rectify traits within myself, like forgiving others, forgiving my past, knowing that God forgave me for my past, and knowing that I was WORTHY to be in the positions that he will put me in. God qualifies those who are called. I had to learn to trust God and not in man or myself for my prosperity. The woman I was with my ex-boyfriend was not his fault but was just the role I played because I had a "people-pleasing" tendency. This caused me to not focus on myself but only to adhere to others' feelings and emotions. I did it because I placed my worth in knowing that others loved me. Not understanding that because God loves me unconditionally, I should not fight to earn the love of others. Their love should not validate my value in myself. Even though caring for others and loving all of God's children is a great trait, me doing it as a means for validation of myself is wrong. My value and who I am was settled at the cross as God loved me so much; he gave his only son, Jesus, to die for my sins.

John 3:16-17 NIV: *"For God so loved the world that he gave his one and only Son, that whoever believes in him shall not perish but have eternal life. For God did not send his Son into the world to condemn the world, but to save the world through him."*

God needed me to cultivate my gifts in ministry to help empower his children into purpose. My capacity to love wholeheartedly and my wisdom would allow me to bless others and bring forth love and prosperity to the world. I realized that doing God's will by helping and caring for others was the right way. Doing it for validation of myself was wrong. I could not accomplish the woman I needed to become while staying in the relationship that I was in. I needed a season of singleness to cultivate the things in my life that I was afraid of doing, like starting a business, writing a book, and thinking that I could accomplish the impossible. I have always played it safe, and God wanted me to operate on faith and not fear. So, I had to step outside of my comfort zone and pursue purpose. This was hard for me because I use to cling to having control and being independent, but it was caused by insecurity and abandonment issues. I realized that I never had control. I have influence and responsibilities, but only God has control. Even when the enemy tries to attack me, he does not have control. He can only have what I allow him to have. That is why I had to understand the power and authority God gave me through his word. There is power in the tongue and mind. The enemy can only corrupt me if I allow his corruption. If I see sorrow, I speak joy and prosperity because I have that authority/influence. This gives me peace. I needed to become the person that God intended for me to be, and at the time, it required making sacrifices that only God could help me endure. He advised me that the company I was keeping with guys from my "past" would only delay my purpose and progress. He knew that they were hindering me from building my faith by relying on him because they were safeguards. I had them in place because I knew they cared about me so much to always be there for me.

Taking the time to cultivate the inner version of myself that needed to be activated was a process God held my hand through every step of the way. God put me through a season of dealing with my past traumas, forgiving those who did me wrong, and understanding who I am based on his word. I had to tell myself all the things that I could accomplish with God and all the authority that I had over my life. I believe God wanted me to take the time to realize all these things that I would not have taken the time to realize being in a relationship. I got comfortable and wanted to focus my attention on my relationship and not on the things of God. Singleness is a season for self-reflection and self-awareness. It is not that while you are in a relationship you should be trying to figure out who you are. If you do not know who you are, how would you know what you are supposed to look for in a significant other or spouse? Do not pray for things that God delivered you from. Pray to God to show you the way so that you do not ask for the things that could hinder your purpose.

In 2020, COVID-19 caused the whole world to stop. During this time, COVID brought on different scenarios: job loss, self-reflection, God's grace, and blessings, work from home, and kids schooling from home. My COVID "world stopping" experience happened in 2019. For the first time in my life, since I was 15, I was two months without employment. For someone like myself who always needed to be in control, I sought validation in my employment status and accolades. God needed me to stop and take time to focus on him. I learned that he was in control, and he shifted my mindset to understand who he was. I believe he did this to give my testimony to everyone this year to help them get the revelation and understanding of God. He wants us to move in purpose. He wants us to know him and understand that he loves us so that we do not waste the rest of our lives pursuing things that would ultimately never satisfy us, like people-pleasing. God wants the best for us. He wants to see us win, but first, we must trust him to get us there. TRUST THE PROCESS.

After reading the story of Joseph, I wondered, "why did God give Joseph such great gifts that he was not ready for?" and "why did he allow him to see his future?" After reading Soul care by Rob Reimer, I gained much clarity. Joseph was immature, proud, and sought validation from the favoritism that his parents showed him compared to his brothers.

It made me realize that God's gifts are not something earned but what God has already placed in us. When God gave him the dream, it was to show Joseph what his future could be. Joseph was never supposed to tell his brothers and boast about it, but he did it, and that is how he ended up a slave. Rob Reimer also explained how Joseph's father made for him the same robe, which made Joseph proud, was the same robe that was ripped by the Potiphar's wife when she accused Joseph of raping her.

This situation landed Joseph in prison. Joseph endures a lot on his path before reaching success, but he had to experience it all because God needed Joseph to get rid of his bad traits. Joseph needed to lose his immaturity, pridefulness and validation-seeking tendencies. God needed Joseph to renew his mind and to hold on to the vision that God gave him while he experienced his pressing season. God wanted Joseph to hold on to his promises, so it made him seek God more and have faith in God. Joseph, through his journey as a slave, received favor from God in every position he earned. God did this to humble Joseph and to help develop that relationship with God as his father. This process pressed Joseph like an olive to develop the anointing oil from God when he became second in command to the King. While in prison, Joseph had a lot of alone time with God, and God could renew his mind and heart. He went from the immature, self-loathing teenager to an obedient humble man who could lead a nation. Joseph's experience resonated so much with me because I experienced a similar path. My experience in 2019 put me through a series of events that lead to the breakdown of my worldly views and a breakthrough of God's love and will for my life. I have gained humility, faith, and obedience during my pressing season, and I know my next step will be leadership and kingdom-based opportunities.

After I transitioned to singleness in 2020, God took the opportunity to resurface some of my past childhood traumas that my mind suppressed over the years. These experiences were traumas I have not thought about in the past 5 -10 years of my life. They say even though the mind forgets, the body remembers. It took me by surprise to see how many unresolved issues I had with other people. These issues shaped my perception when I encountered strangers or when I was trying to establish a deep connection with others. While I ministered to people, I realized that God wanted me to tell my story to others, but before he could allow me to, I would have to resolve my issues. While I told my stories to people, I realized that it was therapeutic for me and provided revelations for others. During the season where God revealed my traumas, he also took the time to remind me of who I am and how my past did not define me. I had to do some real soul care. Through my process of healing and renewing my mind, God sent a word through a prophet to let me know that my past was all forgiven and that he loves me. He reassured me of how those issues of my past will never happen to me again (the planted seeds of the enemy). As God proclaimed it from the prophet, I felt the Holy Spirit doing divine healing in my heart and soul so that I can let go of the baggage that was keeping me bound. My life experiences used to shape the way I saw myself and how it made me have this "people-pleasing" trait, but not anymore. I took back control of my life from the enemy and put it firmly in God's hands.

What people do not understand is that it is a mindset change that we must undergo. You must understand that no one can have power over you that you do not give to them.

God gave us free will, so if the King of Kings does not control us, we should not allow the enemy to overpower us. If you always approach any situation with the mindset of: "all things are working for my good," "no weapon formed against me shall prosper," or "In any situation, I will always be victorious." No situation can come before you that you cannot triumph over. When you have that kind of mindset, you are a force to be wrecking with. God gave us the authority on this Earth when Jesus died for our sins. God gave us the Holy Spirit, as a source of his power, within us. Some may not want that mindset because they are fearful of having to confront trauma or an enemy, but that is the mindset required to live a fruitful life. As you read the Bible, you will see how God reassures us of who we are and the kind of power and authority we have on this Earth. Until you understand that YOU have power and authority, through God, you will continuously allow other factors to take charge in your life when you are the one that is supposed to lead. Everything that happens to you, even when the enemy tries to attack you, you must learn that no weapon formed against shall prosper, and do not let it consume you because all things are working for your good.

Romans 8:28 NIV: *"And we know that in all things God works for the good of those who love him, who have been called according to his purpose."*

Contrary to popular belief, people do not go to hell because of sin; they go to hell because they do not believe in Christ. As Christ died so that we can have eternal life, God sent him because he loved us so much and did not want us to succumb to the will of the devil. God wanted to restore authority to us, his children so that we can inherit our birthright and live life in his abundance of blessings. The death and resurrection of Christ allowed for us not to be measured by our sins but given grace in God's eyes. If you have not accepted God as your Lord and savior, just recite the scripture below over your life and watch Heavens rejoice, for God has been waiting for you all along. No one is perfect, and God knows and loves you where you are at. God is madly in love with you. He just wants a relationship with you. He wants to help heal you and restore you to your exalted position as a joint heir with Christ Jesus. You do not have to try to live up to other people's standards. He just wants you.

If you would like to give yourself to Christ today, it is very easy, just speak these words below and know that Heaven is celebrating your salvation today, your true Father is Proud of you:

Romans 10:9-10 NIV *"If you declare with your mouth, "Jesus is Lord," and believe in your heart that God raised him from the dead, you will be saved. 10 For it is with your heart that you believe and are justified, and it is with your mouth that you profess your faith and are saved."*

KINGDOM ENTREPRENEUR TESTIMONY

When we go through issues with God on our side, we show others how beneficial it is to believe in the God we serve. When he restores us, we give our testimonies to bring awareness to the masses on how faith leads to miracles. When the enemy attacks us, with God on our side, everything that was lost will be restored tenfold. Our testimonies are like Jesus' parables. It is used to help others relate and receive a revelation from God. Then, people can be restored to the kingdom and have everlasting life.

Matthew 13:10-17 NIV: "*The disciples came to him and asked, 'Why do you speak to the people in parables?' He replied, 'Because the knowledge of the secrets of the kingdom of heaven has been given to you, but not to them. Whoever has will be given more, and they will have an abundance. Whoever does not have, even what they have, will be taken from them. Therefore, I speak to them in parables.*"

In 2020, I cannot believe the miracles God blessed me with. June 2020 was the month I moved out of the leased house with my ex-boyfriend and embarked on my season of singleness. I put all my belongings in storage and started to roommate with my dear friends (I love you, ladies). God told me only to take the necessities because he will restore all that I have lost tenfold. God told me that I needed to make provisions in my life and get my house "in order" to receive his divine purpose for my life. He told me that the man I was with was not able to pursue purpose with me. Not every rib is my rib. In translation, I was not his Eve. God told me that even though it looks scary to start over, just trust in him and have faith that he will guide me, protect me, and provide for me during all my seasons. This is my testimony: God is not a man, that he should lie to; neither the son of man, that he should repent. He always keeps his word and I never know how it would look to follow God, but I know it is always worth it in the end.

The scary part about asking God to guide you is that you must be prepared for whatever that looks like because his thoughts are not our thoughts and his ways are not our ways. Faith in his works brings peace and security during any season. I can truly say that I do not regret my decision to let him lead. Faith in him got me the promotion, the multiple streams of income, a beautiful apartment with a lake view, and free furniture. I also grew in confidence, healing, humility, soul care/self-awareness, and the revelations that my life served a purpose. I am so grateful for what he has brought me through, and every time I face a new challenge, I know that if he is done before, He will always and forever do it again for me. He is the Same God! During my singleness, God taught me to place more value on myself because my sins, past, and values were all settled at the cross. He taught me that when a believer partners with God, any barrier can be broken and that nothing in this world can separate me from his love, not death nor life. I took a chance on God because I know all he has gotten me through. Even though this one sounded crazy, at first, I put my trust in him to get me through, and he has never failed. He has blessed me in abundance as I pursue my dreams of being a kingdom entrepreneur.

I

PLANTED SEEDS OF THE ENEMY

As God says, in 1 Corinthians 10, he shall not put more on you than you can bear. The enemy does not follow that same rule. The enemy comes to steal, kill, and destroy, so it is not for a lesson when he attacks you or distracts you. It is to take you out as a competition. So, when he gives you a distraction that seems overwhelming and seems like something you cannot handle, it is not God testing you. It is the enemy attacking you. So, you must know the difference between a lesson that needs to be learned for your personal growth and a distraction that is meant to destroy your purpose.

1 Corinthians 10:13 NIV: "No temptation has overtaken you except what is common to mankind. And God is faithful; he will not let you be tempted beyond what you can bear. But when you are tempted, he will also provide a way out so that you can endure it."

Hope is a weapon that helps us build our faith. The devil comes to take our hope so that we lose faith in God. He takes away hope and instills pain and suffering. The adversary will fight against your holiness in your younger years. He plans to make you incapable of living a holy life. Satan would love to impart seven activities to you during your youth because it is the most vulnerable and impressionable years of any person's life. When he succeeds in planting these seeds in you, you will fail to stay holy for the remainder of your life if you are not intentional. Pornography, rape, fornication, masturbation, molestations, abuse, and homosexuality are the seven seeds that Satan would like to infect us with. The bad thing is that the burning sexual appetite takes away our spirituality and perverts our perception of sex. With all your heart and might, you must combat those desires. Now passion with your spouse is fine, but outside of marriage, the devil uses this as a gateway sin to access us and plant seeds like insecurities, jealousy, etc. The soul ties we have from premarital sex leave us giving parts of our souls to others and taking on the part of someone else's. We do not think to find out someone's heart before sex, but the damage is done after the act is performed. It also makes it harder to date and pursues relationships afterward because you have that lingering sexual attachment to your previous partners. You start to compare your current situation to your past. The worst thing you can do to mess up something special is to compare it to something or someone else. We tend to never stay in the moment with our significant others because we linger on our past due to these soul ties.

Here are my stories of how the enemy planted seeds of sin in me while I was younger. My mom kept me sheltered (away from the harms of society) up until high school. She wanted to instill the right values and character traits into me before she started explaining what she experienced in the world and she taught me who God was. I appreciate her dearly for this. She was doing everything she could to raise me right, but she could not control things that I did not reveal to her. As sex was not discussed in my household, my mother did the best she could based on what she was taught. Churches today are becoming more aware and are promoting parents to talk about the hard topics with their kids, but I was raised in the early 2000s. After my mom and dad separated, I would only visit my father after Church on Sundays. My father was very trusting of me, but he did not know the devil would use that trust against him. Growing up living with my mother, we did not have cable because it was not in the budget. Who would have known that no cable growing up would put a wrench in the devil's plans of planting the seeds of pornography into me? However, at my dad's house, he had cable, and even though he would put the channel on cartoons, he was not always supervising me. While he was outside and I got bored, I would start to scroll through the channels. I stumbled upon pornography and did not know how it would affect me. As it says in Proverbs 4, our eye and ear gates are important and must be guarded.

Proverbs 4:20–22 NIV: "My son, pay attention to what I say; turn your ear to my words. Do not let them out of your sight, keep them within your heart; for they are life to those who find them and health to one's whole body."

The seed was planted, and I learned masturbation through what I witnessed on the screen. I knew sex before marriage was wrong, but I have never heard anything about masturbation, so I did it all in secret. The second seed that the devil planted in me was homosexuality. As a child, my sister was the children's ministry program leader. She would plan fun field trips and events for the children's ministry program at our church. There was one teenage girl in the children's ministry program. She was supposed to be in the youth ministry (teenagers) program, but she wanted to be taught by my sister. My sister understood God's love, and it showed in her teachings. My sister was an amazing teacher, and she instilled values, character, and God's love into me. I am grateful for her every day. They would not allow my sister to lead the youth ministry because she was a woman, so this teenage girl decided to stay in the children's ministry program. One day after coming back from a field trip to a water park, all the kids came to my mom's house, and one by one, we would wait our turn to take a shower. While I was in the shower, probably 7 years old, a teenage girl

CHRIST RENEWED EVERYTHING ABOUT ME - 13

came in the shower with me and exposed me to homosexuality (seed planted). Then the seed was cultivated when I exposed my best friend to it, and we were now "friends with benefits." I do not hold anything against that teenage girl because she was just as confused and ignorant as I was. We did not know any better, but we knew that having sex with a man was a sin, so we thought this was our loophole. We were young, and the devil took advantage of our ignorance.

In the church, we were taught not to have premarital sex, which required a male and female body part, so I thought that if I pursued a woman, I would not be having sex, just some arousing fun. I thought it was my loop whole for my sexual lust release without penetration. The moment when my Godfather caught me at church fooling around with my best friend, at the time, he told me what I was doing was bad and never to do it again. I felt so much ashamed, and I did everything to stop dealing with girls. Instead, I turned to pornography and my imagination because no one would find out what I was doing in secret by myself. All the sexual appetite from masturbation and pornography, not to mention my "people-pleasing" tendency and having a sexually active boyfriend, lead me to have sex at age 15. Switching to physical sex with men took away my desire for a woman, and it made me realize that I only wanted a woman for the wrong reasons. I did not appreciate the physical features God gave me, and it made me desire the features of other women. When I reached that revelation, my desire to be with women was gone. My first partner was a good person. It made me feel comfortable with having sex with future boyfriends after he and I broke up. My logic was if the guy was good to me and was my boyfriend, I did not mind having sex. Understanding that it hurt God to have premarital sex, I would tell God that the guy would be my future husband. That excuse because redundant after boyfriend number three. This allowed my conscience to be okay with having premarital sex because I would only do it with my "future husband." Now, I choose celibacy, and it is an intentional decision every day. God blessed me with the gift of writing, and the devil knew that if he attacked my mind with his seeds of perversion, I would not be able to write and release the word of God. That is why this season of my celibacy was crucial to my ability to write these words because I was canceling out the flesh and the thoughts of perversion/ lust, and I was amplifying God's will through the Holy Spirit in me.

2 Timothy 2:22 NIV: "Flee the evil desires of youth and pursue righteousness, faith, love, and peace, along with those who call on the Lord out of a pure heart."

The enemy uses different tactics for everyone, but he does nothing new under the sun. Therefore, being in a community is so important. You may find someone who went through a similar season to you, and they can help identify the works of the Lord versus the devil's tactics. They can help you to overcome the sin pattern. The enemy never wins because God is the author of our story. When the devil does everything in his power to attack you, do not look at it as "why me?" Do not get caught up in the victimizing role. Instead, realize that your purpose is so great that he must attack you at all different angles to ensure that you fail. He cannot have you obtaining the divine destiny God has for you. You may be the shift in the world that causes great change and positive impact. To avoid us finding who we are, he attacks us. He attacks us when we least expect it because it leaves a deeper scar. When times get hard or things are not going your way, just remember that the devil only attacks those who pose a threat to his mission and not those on his side. They have no value to him. Anyone who finds out who they truly are in Christ is a threat because God created us all with a divine purpose that can easily overthrow the devil's plans. The devil can only secure your fate in hell if you do not know who you are or who God is to you. We are joint-heirs with Christ Jesus. Us being born makes us an automatic threat to the devil's plans, so at birth, he does everything in his power to corrupt or pervert us so that we remain lost. God allowed me to become trained in Adverse Childhood Experiences.

I realized that no matter the current social or economic status someone may have, everyone went through some form of trauma planted in their life by the devil to pervert or corrupt us. The devil tries to plant these seeds when we are most vulnerable, typically when we are children, because we cannot walk away or avoid the situation when we are young. Some may recover from it; some have never recovered and are a product of what happened to them as a child. This helped me to realize that the enemy attacked everyone in some form. However, God is equally working against the devil's attacks to ensure his children discover him and our true identities. The devil will come against anyone who can disrupt his mission, so when he keeps attacking you, just remind yourself that it is a clear indication that your purpose and your future hold great value, so push through.

Understanding the strategies of the enemy is crucial in overcoming spiritual warfare and building a forgiving heart. When you get into that argument with your friend or family member, you must ask yourself, who is truly attacking you? We know how to talk all about how someone's actions made us react, but what if we took a second not to react but discover WHO is behind the attack. What is causing the attack? The enemy can use someone closest to you to hurt you because he spends his time placing thoughts and suggestions in our minds from unresolved issues or insecurities we do not rectify. It is never random; it tends to be built up of unresolved issues between two people that he uses as a weapon to form the ultimate betrayal or offense. Let us talk about how the devil uses people when they are mad; when we are upset with someone, the devil normally just gives suggestions that we tend to act on in our anger. The moments where we blackout and cannot recall what happened are when the enemy takes over us, making people think you are possessed or "they saw the devil in you." Technically, it is true. Now, not every time we act out means we are possessed. It is more of the suggestions that we tend to act on because of the enemy. The best way to rectify that is by not seeking vengeance, you must be intentional within every moment of anger. As God says in Psalm 4, "Be angry but do not sin" because being mad is not a sin but seeking vengeance is a sin.

A generational curse can only be broken if we bring them into the light and overcome them. By understanding them and overcoming them, we can teach our kids how to overcome curses/sin. This requires allowing issues to be brought to the light because keeping things in the dark allows the enemy to continue to prey on you and use this sin against you and your family. When the LORD God said, "It is not good for the man to be alone," in Genesis 2:18, he also meant in terms of inner battles. You should never fight them alone. Seek help and allow God to surround you with the right people who can help you find deliverance from the enemy's GRIP on your life. Even though the curse was passed to the next generation, it does not mean the curse is done with you. The demonic stronghold will remain with you as well because the devil must secure your fate in hell as well as your children. The devil's fate is secured in hell, so he tries to secure our (God's children) fate in hell if he can. That is his main goal because misery loves company. The generational curse is a demonic spirit that follows you and puts situations in your past to expose you to sin (plant the seed) and cultivate it by having you act on the sin through living in sin. My friend once told me how a past relative performed the rituals of passing on the generational curse at the burial site. Before the family would arrive, she would do a ritual that would allow the demonic spirit to wait for the arrival of the next of kin so he can now attach himself to them. This is not the only way a generational curse is passed, but I believe this opened my eyes to understanding that there are no limits to the devil's plot. He would go to great lengths to plant the seed.

Ultimately, you cannot avoid a generational curse from pursuing you. However, you can defeat a generational curse. Like a bully, you cannot avoid the bully because the bully would eventually find you and attack you. You will have to spend your whole time living in fear if you do nothing. However, once you stand up to the bully and defeat them, the bully backs down, and you no longer must live in fear. You can even work to protect others from the bully or teach them what you know so they can also be victorious. Once you defeat the generational curse in your family, you can now develop generational wisdom and protection which is greater than wealth. I decided to confront my family's generational curses. They ran in my family until it ran into me! No more will this demonic spirit torment my life and DEFINITELY NOT the lives of my future children. One thing I have noticed is people do not understand that their children are their image-bearers. What you hate, your child will hate. You cannot assume all kids rebel and become a better version of you. Most children replicate their parents' ideas and beliefs in their core. When you have a narrow view of race, gender, or other people's belief, then do not be shocked to see the children you raise. They become you whether you speak your beliefs or not because your actions show it.

Thou Shall Not Fear

I began understanding that the devil is a modern-day bully. With a bully, the only way to defeat them is to stand up to them. We must understand that it is not a battle that we are fighting because God already defeated him. All he does is torment God's children when we think that we are not capable of overpowering him. Once we understand our authority, then we can rebuke him. You cannot avoid the bully; you must stand firm and defend yourself and put the bully in his place. What I do is fight him with the word of God because the word of God is our sword. God's word reminds us of who we are and the authority we have, so it is good to stay in his word. I now know how to fight fire with fire versus thinking I had no power or authority over him. Earth is a neutral turf where good and evil inhabit. I now understand that the power within me can rebuke evil because my God is greater than all things are Earth.

Ephesians 6:17 NIV: "*Take the helmet of salvation and the sword of the Spirit, which is the word of God.*"

Hebrews 4:12 NIV: "*For the word of God is alive and active. Sharper than any double-edged sword, it penetrates even to dividing soul and spirit, joints and marrow; it judges the thoughts and attitudes of the heart.*"

I learned that God gave us the Holy Spirit as a gift to his children. He wanted us to know that we have all the power to defeat the enemy, heal the sick, and declare with our mouths change for any situation. The Holy Spirit is God's power within us to conquer against the enemy and exercise our birthright as joint-heirs with Christ. An heir is a person inheriting and continuing the legacy of a predecessor. This means, as joint-heirs with Christ, we are granted access to all the riches and power of God. We must not let the devil take away our power anymore and fight our flesh. We are spiritual beings and what hinders us is our flesh. We must fast and understand that we are greater than our flesh. Temptation only works if you allow your flesh to have power over you. We must use our flesh to fulfill God's will on Earth and not allow our flesh to control us. The enemy takes pleasure in our demise.

Zechariah 4:6 NIV: "*So he said to me, "This is the word of the Lord to Zerubbabel: 'Not by might nor by power, but by my Spirit,' says the Lord Almighty.*"

God is on our side, and since he is higher than evil, we trample over evil. But we cannot do that if we do not believe that we are Who We are in Christ. What spoke volumes to me was understanding that the disciples could cure the sick, rebuke the evil, etc., with the Holy Spirit. It made me understand that there is power in what I believe and speak. Therefore, the enemy attacks the mind. Our minds can confine us physically, and this is what the devil wants. As we stay stagnant, he continues to torment others, and we stay imprisoned in this life of hopelessness and suffering. He makes you blame God for this, but it is all his doing. Faith means believing in what you cannot see. A positive mindset helps you to believe in the impossible. As Pastor Mike Todd says, "It is only crazy until it happens." Do not limit God because he is limitless. Do not limit your dreams because you are not bound to your current situation. Nothing can stop you but YOU. The enemy uses your mind against you by showing your fears and disparity all around you to take away your hope. Let us start with learning who we are in Christ and building our faith in God.

Understand that God wanted us to prosper. Like when a child leaves their parents' home, he wants to see you stand on your own. He gave you everything you need for life and godliness through his word. His power is already inside of you. Use his word to activate and cultivate your power. It is already inside you, but you need to believe that it is. Change your mindset and advance your life. In due time you would understand the true power and greatness of God. The beautiful thing about the Bible is that it is a history lesson. It is also a love story about God and man. As in any great relationship, there are ups and downs, but overall, there is love. Respect and forgiveness are what produce longevity. The book of Matthew is the foundation of Christianity because it was the period when Jesus gave all his knowledge to us in the three years of his Ministry. As the other disciples' chapters explain their perspectives and experiences, I believe it is important to understand what Jesus saw for us. Then James, Proverbs, and Ecclesiastes. We must also see how his disciples used the gifts of the Holy Spirit to do God's will on Earth.

This foundation will help all new believers and seasoned believers understand God's will for his people to be image bearers on Earth. Provide hope, love, grace, mercy, and all his fruitful spirits to the lost and found. We remain on Earth with those who may not believe because our goal is not to condemn them but to salvage the Lost and help them discover themselves in Christ. To assist means that help was requested. We do not force people to change. We love them. Show them that shame and regret and condemnation are not the fruit of the Lord, but love, Mercy, forgiveness, Grace, peace, and prosperity is what God wants for everyone. We must show it to them with our actions so that they can see the love of God through us.

From Paper to Process

I believe what we must understand from this chapter is that we must be vigilant in guarding our children as parents. When we take on the parenting role, we are signing up to be a warrior because we must protect our children from the bad in this world. We must understand how to protect them. Lying or withholding information/ secrets from them is not a way of protection. Transparency builds trust and vulnerability. You want to prepare your child for what they might encounter in this world but explain it in a way that will build courage and not instill fear. Suppose you are not knowledgeable on how to research it? It is best to ask your spiritual leaders. We must create an open communication method with children to assess their shortcomings and prepare them for adulthood properly. We must not think that if we avoid certain topics our child will not find out. This is the wrong way of thinking. If the devil is working vigilantly to plant seeds in your child, not informing your child of what to look out for would only allow the devil the advantage to attack them. Them unaware of what an attack looks like will only set them up for failure. If they were attacked as a child but did not realize it was an attack until they are much older, it could turn their world upside down. They are left feeling depressed, having identity issues (insecurities, low self-esteem, or self-worth), or regret because something was taken from them, and they did not know how precious it was until it was gone. If you inform them of what could happen, they will be alert and avoid adverse childhood experiences. Leaving this in the dark only allows darkness to thrive. Bringing it to the light can help combat the attacks because you will have a chance to do something about it. Like when we teach them how to call the police "call 911" or to "not talk to strangers," we need to teach them about friendships, relationships, sex, generational curses, God, and the Holy Spirit within them. Teach them to guard their hearts with a gate and not a wall, discernment, and knowing themselves and the boundaries that should be in place with their bodies. The sad thing is once the seed is planted, it is cultivated over the years. It is not just one attack but various attacks that develop over the years, and then it makes it harder to reverse, so we must allow kids that space to be vulnerable, especially when they are teenagers. Ask God to pour grace into you because we must be able to hear kids' mistakes and shortcomings and approach them in a way that provides coaching and understanding, just as God provides us as adults.

When we sin and repent, God does not banish or ridicule us. He opens his heart to us and helps us change our ways. No one is perfect, and if you ever have a moment where your child's shortcomings are very disappointing, call your parents and ask your parents about all the crazy things you did as a child. Then humble yourself because no child is perfect. This will help you gain empathy for your child. Even when you may respond unfavorably to your child, and the Holy Spirit or your parent reminds you of what you did, go to your child, and apologize. Explain to them what happened to you, your mistakes, and how you want to help them make better choices. We must stop raising our kids as our parents did, especially if we ended up with trauma growing up. I understand as parents, we may not always have the patience when unexpected issues arise. Everything is a teachable moment, and an apology goes a long way. Just think of how this training will help your grandkids in the future because what you instilled in your child today will be generational. So aside from giving children generational wealth, let us give them generational wisdom and security. That is one thing I admire about my mother; she was very transparent with me, and when I messed up, she gave me grace, and empathy and prayed for me during my formative years (11-17 years old). My mom would tell me about her faults and explain to me about her journey in life. She took great care in preparing me for the world, and I am glad she did.

I was not as open about my lust battle because our family did not talk about sex growing up, but I had values and a moral compass. Since sex before marriage is a sin, it brought me shame to even claim that I was battling it. Instead, I hid it, and the devil got the advantage from that. My capacity to love and empathize is based on me guarding my heart with a gate and not a wall. I set boundaries that did not cause me to change who I am. Of course, I am not perfect, so I did have some that hurt me, but God restores me through healing. It made me aware of boundaries, and eventually, through salvation, God helped me forgive those who have wronged me, and I am free. My heart is open, and I love how God loves. I am still working on patience and love when it comes to driving in Florida's traffic. No one's perfect.

Both parents should be involved in matters concerning the child. The father is the leader, and the wife is the helper, so when they must engage in discussions with their child, it should be the father leading and the mother's support. Of course, a woman can always lead the conversation, and the father supports her because teamwork is key. No parent should be negligent in their child's life because you brought that child into this world with the sole purpose of making sure they were raised properly. You want your child to be comfortable going to both parents with issues and understand that they will get the best advice from either. Work together to raise your children because the devil preys on the children with neglectful parents, and it takes both perspectives to raise a child. Because mothers are usually nurturers, children sometimes embrace the moral aspect of their mothers. It is a woman's gift, so it is easier for a child to be vulnerable with their mom. This does not mean the father cannot obtain that vulnerability with the child. Like my mother, you would have to be a nurturer in a single-parent household but not an enabler. It requires trust, but trust is built over time with wisdom, compassion, grace, and the ability to forgive. The beauty of this is that we can plant that seed and instill the right values in them early on because we raise the child. Then we cultivate the seed of trust. However, sometimes we do not learn these things until after a child's formative years, so we must work harder to regain our child's trust and vulnerability. It would be like getting to know a stranger. It takes work to build trust because it is so fragile. It is not impossible, but it is necessary to help your child talk about what they struggle with in secret. We never know the extent of the damage until it is too late, so be more proactive than reactive.

2

OVERCOMING SIN PATTERNS & GENERATIONAL CURSES

After reading Soul Care by Dr. Rob Reimer, it was one of the foundational books on my spiritual journey. This book and the verses from Deliver Me (This Is My Exodus) Song by Donald Lawrence, below, spoke to my soul:

"When you become a believer
Your spirit is made right
And sometimes, the soul doesn't get to notice
It has a hole in it
Due to things that have happened in the past
Hurt, abuse, molestation
But we wanna speak to you today and tell you
That God wants to heal the hole in your soul
Some people's actions are not because their spirit is wrong, But it is because the past has left a hole in their
soul."

When we find God and salvation, we are made new creatures in Christ. We can begin to use the authority and gifts God has already given us through the Holy Spirit that is activated within us. The Holy Spirit helps us overcome any and everything on this Earth because God gives us power. Christ died so that we can live and receive the Holy Spirit. I did want to take the time to provide some context and provide an understanding that everyone has a Soul and a Spirit within them. Even though the Spirit has been made new through Christ, the Soul has not. The Soul is the part of us that holds on to the pain and joys we experience in life. The soul is the part of us that harbors our behaviors (in this case, sin patterns). That is why you can see a very influential and talented Pastor who may struggle with infidelity. I say that to give you an example of how God can use the gifts he instilled in us to save lives, but our Souls can still be struggling with our sinful behaviors. The gift is instilled in us, but we are still human, so we must learn to separate them (Man and Gift). We must learn not to judge but to pray for all are spiritual leaders and all children of God. Everyone has a gift, so we are all equal no matter what our gifts are. Forgiveness is a crucial step in your walk with God because it allows you to become free of bondage and love how God loves. Since we do not address the issues we have in our souls, we do not experience the fullness of the new life that we receive through salvation. Ideally, God would prefer both the man and the gift to be more aligned, but sometimes we overlook issues. Even though we are saved, our issues do not just work themselves out.

Even as we read about Moses in Exodus, we can see that he was a gifted and favored man that God used to do great things. But what we did not notice was the issues Moses had, and sadly those issues kept him from getting to see the Promised land. Pastor Dharius Daniels helped me to realize that his anger issues and seeking validation from the people of Israel made him trapped in an invisible prison. It kept him from seeing his full potential in God. As God wanted to strike down the people of Israel, Moses begged for mercy on them. The same people who did not appreciate him caused his moments of anger towards them. They did not value his sacrifices which caused him to act out of character. It showed that he was seeking validation from the people who were his assignment. He was not obedient to God. He was saving the people so they would love him and not because God told him to.

Moses had issues that stemmed from being adopted and having to choose between the family he was raised by or his people. Rooted in internal conflict, his impulsive anger caused him to kill the king's guard for punishing the Israelite slave. When the Israelites did not accept him after they found out about his sacrifices, he fled due to fear of the Egyptians finding out. As you can see, unresolved childhood issues can manifest themselves into poor traits as adults (people-pleasing). His value was based on his people's love and not the love of God, and he did not see that as a problem. But God did. Moses was not raised by his biological parents, and the family that raised him (Pharaoh) enslaved his people and killed them, so he did not know where he fits in. Throughout the books of Exodus to Deuteronomy, you can see how he sought validation from man, and God telling him he was worthy was not enough for him. He was a people pleaser, and when the people rejected him, it made him angry, and his actions cost him the promised land. God could not use someone who is bound. Moses not dealing with his issues would have been a liability if he went to the promised land.

Deuteronomy 32:51–52 NIV: "This is because both of you broke faith with me in the presence of the Israelites at the waters of Meribah Kadesh in the Desert of Zin and because you did not uphold my holiness among the Israelites. Therefore, you will see the land only from a distance; you will not enter the land I am giving to the people of Israel."

This is also why the Israelites were left in the wilderness for 40 years because the current generation was trapped in their invisible prison. Apart from disobedience, they also had unresolved issues and could not understand that God was their source or the concept of faith in him. They did not fully believe in God's power and, in turn, were very disobedient. As I read through the book of Exodus to Numbers, all I could do is tell God, "I am sorry." As I look back on my sins, I am truly grateful Jesus died so that I could live. God tossed my sins into the sea of forgetfulness. God could not use the current generation of Israelites to fulfill what needed to be done. Their journey required them to conquer the promised lands from their current inhabitants. God was going to send them on missions to conquer the world, which would require faith and obedience because they would be up against giants and dangerous people. The only way they could win is by believing that God would make them victorious because God favored them. Faith is a prerequisite.

Numbers 20:10–12 NIV: "He and Aaron gathered the assembly together in front of the rock, and Moses said to them, "Listen, you rebels, must we bring you water out of this rock?" Then Moses raised his arm and struck the rock twice with his staff. Water gushed out, and the community and their livestock drank. But the Lord said to Moses and Aaron, "Because you did not trust in me enough to honor me as holy in the sight of the Israelites, you will not bring this community into the land I give them."

God loves us so much that he takes us as we are (broken) and helps repair us. However, God is a gentleman. God will not force your transformation; you must want it for yourself. But do not feel you need to be whole for God to love you or help you. Man sets that requirement, but God is here today to remind you that he wants you AS YOU ARE. In him, he will teach you love and self-worth. "My value and my sins were settled at the Cross through salvation in Christ!" Utter those words every time someone tries to remind you of the old you or if the devil makes you think you are unworthy in your mind. You do not need a man to love you. Remember that God loves you, and he knew you were worth dying for.

John 3:16-17 NIV: "*For God so loved the world that he gave his one and only Son, that whoever believes in him shall not perish but have eternal life. For God did not send his Son into the world to condemn the world, but to save the world through him.*"

To go through a transformation, you must experience a revelation, and both steps require intentional actions (choice). When someone sins, people tend to focus on the sin versus what caused the sin. Sin is a symptom. There is an underlying disease. An example of a Disease would be considered being Molested, Raped, or Abandonment issues. They may give symptoms of jealousy, insecurity, narcissism, unfaithfulness, selfishness, gossip and speaking down to others/intimidation, people-pleasing, be judgmental, needing validation, or the need to perform. So, taking the time to understand the disease would benefit you more than telling them to stop displaying certain attributes of the disease. Yes, it is good to worship and read the word of God, but you must also take the time to reflect and resolve the diseases of the Soul (The heart of the matter) through prayer and meditation with God so that you can become whole and more like Jesus.

Matthew 12:34-35 NIV: "*You brood of vipers, how can you who are evil say anything good? For the mouth speaks what the heart is full of. A good man brings good things out of the good stored up in him, and an evil man brings evil things out of the evil stored up in him.*

Matthew 15:18-20 NIV: "*But the things that come out of a person's mouth come from the heart, and these defile them. For out of the heart come evil thoughts—murder, adultery, sexual immorality, theft, false testimony, slander. These are what defile a person, but eating with unwashed hands does not defile them.*"

God wants to remind us that nothing we do can separate us from his love:

Romans 8:38-39 NIV: "For I am convinced that neither death nor life, neither angels nor demons, neither the present nor the future, nor any powers, neither height nor depth, nor anything else in all creation, will be able to separate us from the love of God that is in Christ Jesus our Lord."

God loves us and wants all his children to return to him, and through repentance, it is possible. Do not let anyone condemn you as Jesus said; in John 8, the ones WITHOUT sin should cast the first stone. As that person judges you, they are also sinning by judging. So, rest assured that everyone needs help:

John 8:7 NIV: "When they kept on questioning him, he straightened up and said to them, "Let anyone of you who is without sin be the first to throw a stone at her."

No one has earned the grace of God; it was given to us through Christ's death and resurrection. Learn how to do right through his word in the New Testament. It will help you to focus on what to do so you can live a righteous life. Jesus came to provide clarity to his children and to redeem us from the hand of the enemy.

Matthew 18: 6-9 NIV: "If anyone causes one of these little ones—those who believe in me—to stumble, it would be better for them to have a large millstone hung around their neck and to be drowned in the depths of the sea. Woe to the world because of the things that cause people to stumble! Such things must come, but woe to the person through whom they come! If your hand or your foot causes you to stumble, cut it off and throw it away. It is better for you to enter life maimed or crippled than to have two hands or two feet and be thrown into eternal fire. And if your eye causes you to stumble, gouge it out and throw it away. It is better for you to enter life with one eye than to have two eyes and be thrown into the fire of hell."

From Paper to Process

I wanted to share my journey to conquering my flesh with those who had the seed of lust planted at a young age. Staying in God's word and watching sermons on people's experiences with lust helped me to understand that this was not an impossible battle. When I get the urge, reminding myself that it is not satisfying afterward and the shame I felt from condemnation helped me avoid the thoughts. I started to unfollow any provocative pages or people that post too much of their bodies on social media. I switched to more gospel music, during this process, to stay in praise and worship more with God. It helped restore God's promises in my mind, and it started to cleanse my mind of the pervasive thoughts I used to have. As God says to secure the eye and ear gates, I went extreme because I knew this was something I was battling for over a decade. If I wanted to succeed, I would have to sacrifice what seems easy for something a little challenging. I had to go through a period of reprogramming my mind to repurpose my thoughts on things that would bring me fulfillment (purpose and helping others) versus self-gratification. Now that I will overcome it, the devil tries to test my restraint occasionally, but I pass every time by the grace of God. Understanding what triggered me helped me to notice and pivot. No more will I dip my toe into it because that is how the flesh takes you down a rabbit hole, figuratively speaking. I have begun listening to other subtle music genres again, but I stay away from suggestive shows that have sex scenes and just anything that would cause me to want to watch it. It is a rabbit hole effect, so if you stop beforehand, then you would not commit the act. If you have the idea of turning it on or just researching or watching something suggestive, I will choose not to. I asked God to help me, of course, through prayer every time, and I had to build up the tolerance to avoid those things by feeding my spirit and fasting (which kills the fleshly desire) to make my spirit more powerful than my flesh. Sometimes, in my favorite show, there may be suggestive moments, but I skip over them. I do that now since I am recovered. I am not inclined to want to watch porn anymore, and I thank God every day.

Understanding where you are with the exposure to lust is important.

Your feelings for sex are connected to your spirituality. If not properly managed (premarital), it can lead to pain and unwanted attachments. The effects from it, like soul ties, would mean a part of your soul is taken with every person you have sex with. This can also lead to lusting after past partners and so on. The first way to combat lust is to guard your eye and ear gates by stopping yourself from developing those appetites. It is more difficult to regulate lust once you have developed a taste for such sexual things. For example, in pornography, they made things unrealistic. If you try to impose that on your spouse, it will lead to discomforting sexual experiences. Second, you must pray against it for the rest of your life if you have already developed a taste for sexual perversions like pornography, masturbation, and homosexuality. Giving your sexuality an outlet is the third thing to do to combat lust. This outlet will come from marriage, where you will be able to have sexual intercourse regularly. Whatever the case, you will have to intentionally avoid the sin pattern for the remainder of your life. Even in marriage, pornography is not healthy for your marriage. My only concern with option three is that you must still manage your lust because your partner's sex drive may not meet the need. If your lust causes you to value sex in your marriage, you will have to talk with your spouse about your issues' severity. Self-control is important.

2 Corinthians 12:7-9 NIV: *"because of these surpassingly great revelations. Therefore, in order to keep me from becoming conceited, I was given a thorn in my flesh, a messenger of Satan, to torment me. Three times I pleaded with the Lord to take it away from me. But he said to me, 'My grace is sufficient for you, for my power is made perfect in weakness.' Therefore, I will boast more gladly about my weaknesses so that Christ's power may rest on me."*

Understand what your sin patterns are and accept that it is okay that you struggle with them currently. Rome was not built overnight, but God created all things in six days, so do not doubt the power he can give you to overcome your sin patterns. Notice the daily or even monthly recurring sins that make you feel like the enemy just comes into your life, only for a split second, to cause you to sin and condemn yourself. He tries to make you feel ashamed and feel like you are not worth God's love. However, God has always said that he us grace based on Jesus, as he sent Jesus to die for our sins. One thing I would like to point out is that everybody may not have the same sin pattern or are affected by the same triggers. You must find what works for you and understand that it may not work for others around you. Others may not have the same triggers as you, so you cannot shame someone else for not being as cautious as you. Like, for me, my sin pattern was lust through pornography and masturbation. I refrain from looking at suggestive things that would provoke those thoughts or initiate those actions, but my friends could probably watch those things all day and feel nothing from them. I understood what my sin pattern was, and I did what was best for me. I would always allow my friends to do what they wanted to do, and I established boundaries to secure my progress. I know what would provoke me and let them know to be aware and respect the boundaries. If they are truly your friend, they will help you be the better version of yourself by any means.

Matthew 5:30 NIV: "And if your right hand causes you to stumble, cut it off and throw it away. It is better for you to lose one part of your body than for your whole body to go into hell."

As you read Matthew 5:30, some may think Jesus meant it literally, but Jesus taught in parables to help people relate better to his teachings. From my understanding, Jesus was saying to notice your triggers and avoid them. When you realize what your sin pattern is, you will identify the triggers. You figure out what triggers you to think those thoughts or go down that "rabbit hole" where you cannot come back out. Next, you cut those triggers out of your life. In the beginning, it is going to be a little hard, but overall, you learn to live without those things. You will start to see them and improve in your ability to restrain from falling into sin patterns. Always work with God on that as well because he provides strength when we are weary. Stay active in your reading of the word. Start to journal your experience and progress. If you need help, then ask God to help you by showing you ways to improve your ability to resist that sin pattern's temptation. Be intentional every day because you never know when the devil is going to try to tempt you. You must be intentional to know when your trigger is being placed in front of you or if you pursue a certain thing that would cause a trigger for you. It is perfectly fine to say, "Hey, I am going to just pursue other things just for the sake of my purity, sanity, and progress." Do not consult with your flesh to decide what is best for you; we are spiritual beings, and the attacks are spiritually based. You must ask yourself if the sin is worth the shame, the emptiness/meaningless, the pain and feeling of life being depressing/overwhelming.

1 Corinthians 8:9 NIV: "Be careful, however, that the exercise of your rights does not become a stumbling block to the weak."

3

THE POWER OF COMMUNITY

Sisterhood and Brotherhood are an essential part of your Christian journey. They hold you accountable; they relate to you in ways that your spouse and family may not.

Ecclesiastes 4:9-10 NIV: "Two are better than one because they have a good return for their labor: If either of them falls down, one can help the other up. But pity anyone who falls and has no one to help them up."

They are the true blessing in your life; as God said, no man should be alone; he believed we all need a group that would intercede on our behalf and gets us through our trials and tribulations. These individuals will get us through hard-to-break sin patterns (because we all have them at times) and pray with us and for us. They believe in our dreams and remind us who we are when we forget. Pray partners help pray for you when the Devil is tempting you with sin patterns that you have been working to resolve. They can intercede in your life when the devil works all hours of the night to try to set you up for failure. As you confess your sins, it brings your secrets into the light so God can surround you with people who can help guide you.

Colossians 3:13 NIV: "Bear with each other and forgive one another if any of you has a grievance against someone. Forgive as the Lord forgave you."

Pray the Lord surrounds you in the community. This may require letting go of the friends in your life that do not bear any fruit to your life. As God said:

John 15:1-2 NIV: "I am the true vine, and my Father is the gardener. He cuts off every branch in me that bears no fruit, while every branch that does bear fruit, he prunes so that it will be even more fruitful."

It is a true blessing in disguise that we never know until we witness the angels God surrounds us with. Your group can be there to get baptized with you, spend time in Bible study, and evolve together. You are learning more and more about God together and helping remind each other in seasons of pressing and pruning. We learn forgiveness, love, grace, and mercy from his words, and we work every day to be more like Christ as his image-bearers on Earth. Surround yourselves intentionally with people who help you level up and evolve. Network and support each other to where Everyone has their talents they bring to the table. As each one grows in knowledge, they exchange the knowledge at group events and gatherings. Your team/group should come together to form movements that will leave a legacy. Establish companies where each of your team would play a role, whether CEO, CFO, or a board member (because I love a great Non-profit organization). God wants his children to unite and prosper. Let us make spiritual generational wealth because you are brothers and sisters through Christ. Your assignment for tonight is to pray & fast for God to send you your team and to remove those individuals in your life that do not bear you any fruit. Please keep in mind that I am not saying that those people cannot be in your life (some may not make the cut); they just cannot be your "team/group," they will keep you stagnant.

1 Thessalonians 5:11 NIV: "Therefore, encourage one another and build each other up, just as you are doing."

The Importance of Boundaries

God loves us and always wants the best for us. He places the good people into our lives to elevate us in purpose. The devil places the distraction into our lives to deter us from our purpose. When you experience a friendship that is a pure blessing to your life, Thank God for it. He will always bring you stability and love. We get so used to the friends who did not deserve us and may misuse us that we think it is all we can find. This is not true; if we invested in ending unreciprocated friendships, God would fill that position with the right people. Even if that great person were in your life for just a season, God would replace it with someone better. He just wanted to give you the hope you needed by making your paths cross. God knows when we are worried or feeling overwhelmed, so he sends reassurance. Whether it is a dream, prophesy, or in the form of an encounter. When God removes people from your life, it is because he knows their true intentions. He knows that someone will hinder your full potential. We must not put faith in our friendships. We must put our faith in God always to surround us with the right people. He is your source, and so he knows what you need for all seasons that you will endure on this Earth. Trust in his process. God surrounds his children with those who need to be in their life. He knows what is best for us. Some may not understand because they must first accept that God is our Father. He behaves as such. Ideally, he gave us Earthly parents to understand the role he plays in our life. Therefore, when he said we must have faith like a child, he meant that because he is our father. When we are young, we rely solely on our parents, and they always provide for us. Of course, the devil distorts things, and everyone was not allowed to have the ideal mother and father. The devil turns anything pure, from God to negative. Like Sex, God intended for it to be through marriage, but the devil made it premarital and put his spin on it (pornography, masturbation, molestation, rape). However, God does not stop being who he is because of that. Instead, he will help us to see him in a different light. Changing your mindset! He puts us through trust exercises to build our faith in him and then displays his fatherly characteristics so that we can view the role as he intended. The Bible also gives an understanding of God's character as a father to us. Understand that he is our father, and he will show us how he intended for this role to be in our lives. He also teaches us forgiveness towards our Earthly parents who may have "miss the mark." The devil has been at work on humanity from day one, so we must learn to forgive them. His tactics date back for centuries. We must learn his tactics and not fall for the same generational warfare. It reminds me of how Jesus always spoke in parables so that we could understand him better. God did the same, and I slowly begin to understand that.

As relationships are important to our growth, we must place value on establishing boundaries to maintain peace. The devil understands the power in community and works diligently to place offenses in our relationships to have tension/unresolved issues. Our gifts are never a curse if we take the time to learn our gifts. Our personalities and who we are will never harm if we learn to put people in their place. As I will explain more in the "Power of forgiveness" chapter, knowing the difference between an assignment and a friend is important. With an assignment, their ability to reciprocate the love is not required. A school assignment is turned into a professor for a grade. Your job is to turn that person to God so he can redeem their soul. Love them with God's heart, but they are not to have access to you. They are going through a healing and restoration journey; giving them the expectation to love you back is unfair. They can prevent your gifts from bringing blessings to you. Understanding that we cannot change the gifts God gave us will help us to make provisions. Gifts are given without repentance. We must understand Who We are and how God made us cannot be changed internally. I choose to embrace my gifts and established boundaries to protect them. I allow the Holy Spirit to give me discernment on what information I should share with others. This allows me to be fulfilled in the work I do and not be bound by fear of pain/betrayal. My compassion for people and seeing people do great things is my gift. I help to nurture their minds and be that beacon of love. God has brought people into my life that would give me instant access to them. They would divulge their business and not even know me. I used to wonder if there was a sign above my head that said, "vent here." As I started to understand my gift, I realized God placed it on their hearts to "bare it all" with me because he knew I would minister his love and wisdom to them. I also learned the hard way that this gift could affect my dating life. When I was not intentionally dating, I would get emotionally attached to men, which made it harder to determine whether he was the one or not? God had a funny way of showing when a guy was not the one. Therefore, I may come off as very professional with my breakup process... a few trials and errors. I am the light, so God sometimes surrounds me with people with the intention of me helping to elevate them and to show them who God is. I learned it the hard way, but I assure you, I learned it!

The devil tries to use everyone to sin. Even those individuals who think they are not capable of being used. Just remember, if you act in anger, then you have sinned. Once you allow yourself to seek revenge after anger, you are opening that gateway for the enemy to use you to hurt the person you love. Consider that the next time you are thinking of allowing your feelings to lead you into an argument. Think of the risk you are taking by pursuing that. We cannot assume our partner or friend would say the right thing to calm us down. What if they do not consider your feelings and you all exchange words of hurt that you cannot take back? The point is, that we must be intentional. Not everyone has mastered this, but we must be the outliers of the world. Choose to take a moment and regroup to figure out the root cause of the argument and address it with love and kindness. Just allowing the anger or the offense to manifest would just create a series of wrong turns in the relationship. You will be digging a deep hole that would be hard to recover from. Being hungry is not a sin but over-consume is a sin. Being aroused is not a sin, but lusting is a sin, and being angry is not a sin; revenge is a sin. Resting is not a sin but being slothful is. This shows us that the reaction is what counts and not the cause. Let us be intentional by being more self-aware of our triggers and things that would get an unfavorable reaction from us.

Ecclesiastes 7:21-22 NIV: "Do not pay attention to every word people say, or you may hear your servant cursing you— for you know in your heart that many times you yourself have cursed others."

As we are the hands and feet of God's will on Earth, we must place a certain level of value on our relationships. We must be intentional when solving issues. The devil likes to plant seeds of offenses to break alliances. There is strength in numbers. When someone informs you that you have offended them, be mindful; just apologize. Explain that it was not your intention. It is our job to hear each other out and be selfless towards each other. With your friends, you get the best practice for marriage because marriage is truly a selflessness test. We must be okay with apologizing versus getting defensive and not understanding that we cannot control how our actions or words make someone feel. Being right is less important in the relationship, and I think we must get out of the prideful spirit. The devil plants seed in the minds that make us think negatively when someone says something that we took the offensive. If we remind ourselves of others' true intentions, the devil cannot put us against each other. In situations where I need to be blunt with my friends, I like to remind them of my intentions so when an issue happens, they will be inclined to give me the benefit of the doubt. Whenever the enemy is trying to plant that seed in their minds, my friends understand we have an open form of communication. If they want to confront issues, then I highly recommend it. I never want the devil to have the upper hand, so I practice transparency, honesty, and openness. The battle is always internal, so I cannot fight the enemy in my friend's head. I can only remind them who they are and how the devil will do anything in his power to destroy who they are. The enemy has been using us against each other for centuries. That is how he continues his plan, but God has a divine agenda. He plans to unite humanity against the real enemy.

Confession and Confrontation

The power of confession and the power of confrontation is extremely important. When we hold things in, the enemy will try to make us feel like we are not worthy or that the person did it to hurt us. He tries to have a hold on us through our offenses that we do not address or forgive. Without forgiveness, the enemy can continue to have a GRIP on us. He brings up past offenses and causes us to relive them. He wants us to pursue an argument so that he can use us to attack each other. The devil may be one spirit, but he has demons that do his bidding, day in and day out. He has a hold on us when we keep secrets. He reminds us that we are not worthy and condemns us. It is better to confess the sin than to hold it in and live with the mental-spiritual battle that comes with a secret. If we were to confess our sins and repent, it would give us clarity and freedom from the enemy's mind games.

I used to struggle with confrontation because I had the "people-pleasing" mentality that made me feel like if I confronted someone, it would lessen their love for me. A confrontation would sometimes lead to a disagreement, and that would mean they did not love me. I used to seek validation and value in the people I loved. Not anymore. Reading Soul Care helped me to understand that God loves me, and that is all I need. I may want people to love me, but it is not required anymore. I had to be okay with losing friendships due to confrontation. I realized that I needed to understand my value in Christ. My value was settled at the cross, and God loves me with his unconditionally and unwavering heart. I have learned how to confront people by making sure I word things properly to get my point across. The goal is not to offend by using profanity. The best way to approach the situation is to state what happened to you and how it made you feel. Offenses will cause us to resent that person or avoid that friendship so let us intentionally resolve offense with healthy confrontations and confessions. We need to take the time to rectify issues and state how we feel so everyone feels heard. The worst thing to do is hold a grudge for years that manifest into betrayal or hate. It is even more dangerous when we set unspoken expectations that they did not meet, and we are offended. We are holding on to something that they did not even know we were holding on to, and it is not their fault. We never brought it to their attention. Allow them to apologize to you and show you that they value your friendship. Let us not hold on to any more deadweight grudge. Allowing the enemy to use us is not the will of God for our lives. The enemy will try to stir up hate and resentment. Without forgiveness, God cannot completely use us, nor does he hear our prayers as it says in Mark 11:25. The enemy makes sure that if we have offenses and lack forgiveness in our hearts, the Lord cannot completely use us as vessels. We cannot fulfill our purpose in God, which limits our impact on the world. Offense causes people not to trust easily or allow people in that need our help. It can even deter the people God wanted to surround us with to help us fulfill our destiny.

Mark 11:25 NIV: *"And when you stand praying, if you hold anything against anyone, forgive them, so that your Father in heaven may forgive you your sins."*

Understanding who is for you and who is not for you is important when establishing boundaries. God does prune your friend's lists because they did not bear good fruit in your life. Sometimes it can be that person who is secretly jealous of you. God makes sure that you now see that person's personality because he wants you to remove that person. The process is tough but ultimately necessary for you to thrive. I recommend falling in love with the process and not sharing your business with everyone this season. God is trying to make space for the right people to enter your life to take those vacant positions.

From Paper to Process

Before you start praying for the spouse, Pray God surrounds you with the right people so you can start moving toward your purpose. You want to know who you are and what you are supposed to do, so when your spouse comes along, you will know they are the one. I am currently working on starting my brands and moving towards my purpose. God has blessed me with a team. Women from all walks of life who serve him. It is a beautiful thing. Sisterhood is important, and it follows you through your life, especially in marriage. It took me a lot to be where I am today. I sacrificed a lot of people that were not helping me evolve.

As much as it is a little bittersweet, I can now see that I would not find myself without losing them. God knows what he is doing when he prunes your friends. It gives you more time to find new ones that align with the person you must become. You are evolving, and trust; it is beautiful. Our soul holds on to those memories, and trust me when I tell you, my mind sometimes reminisces about my past. I remind myself of what I would have to give up by keeping them, which was myself and my future. It is exciting and scary to make new friends, I know. When someone enters your life, ask God to reveal to you if they are supposed to be there, and he will. God moved me to Orlando in 2017, and I did not know that the various employment opportunities were things I had to experience to meet all the different women I did to form my Circle. I tell you, I would have never thought this would be his plan, but he does use everything in our life (good and bad) for our good. I could talk forever about all the things I experienced (even mistakes) that God has used to better my life. Live life with no regrets. Repent, and God forgives you, and no one can condemn you because he does not. See what you have learned from your experiences to give God the glory.

We need to start facing our problems head-on. I learn that avoiding things or living for others only brings destruction and depression to our lives. During my journey, I realized the power of singleness and moments of solitude with God. When people run to another city or another state to redefine themselves, they must establish boundaries once they return home. When you come back home, you are still held to that same standard of who you used to be. To fully live in your renewed life, you must set boundaries with people and not allow someone to make you question who you have become. Try every day, intentionally, to be a better version of yourself. This is how we establish permanent change. When others try to remind you of who you used to be, you must stand firm in your truth and know who you are. Do not fall into who you used to be. Let people know that those things are not of you anymore. Show people that you have changed for the better and do not need them to hold you to that previous standard. Be okay with making new friends that are more aligned with the person you are now. God will surround you with like-minded people as you pursue him. He wants you to have a community that stands firm with you through every trial, tribulation, and blessing. This is where the boundaries may lead to the loss of friendships. Let them know that this is no longer the path you are pursuing in life. If you hurt someone in the past and encounter them, be mindful and apologize for your past behavior. Forgiveness is something that we should try to spread, and an apology goes along with that. Let us all heal together and pursue purpose.

4

THE POWER OF FORGIVENESS

God's grace and mercy are everlasting and for everyone. The devil's place in Hell is secured. There is no redemption for him because he was an angel in Heaven, and he did wrong. As the Bible states in Matthew 25, Hell was only intended for the Devil and his demons.

Matthew 25:41 NIV: "Then he will say to those on his left, 'Depart from me, you who are cursed, into the eternal fire prepared for the devil and his angels."

As we may ask, "why is the devil not given a second chance?" Consider this... the Angels in Heaven do not have the same chance for grace and mercy as we do on Earth because they are already secured in Heaven with God. They are not tempted like us on Earth. God gave us grace because he understands that we are spirit beings that live in the flesh on Earth. The little chance we had in Eden was cut short because of the devil using our flesh against us. On Earth, our flesh is tempted by evil. The devil lurks on earth trying to secure our fate in Hell with him because misery loves company. God understood that was the devil's strategy once the devil used Adam and Eve to sin. So, Jesus died for our sins to have our names written in the book of life and have everlasting life in Heaven. The death and resurrection of Jesus washed away all our sins and provided us grace from God, which gave us the Holy Spirit's power to overpower our flesh. This was a plot twist the devil did not see coming. We have authority on Earth as God's ambassadors. God understands our flesh can cause us to be manipulated by the devil. Our flesh is weak. God made the requirement for us to return to him so simply because he wants all his children to have a fair chance at redemption and salvation.

As God stated, our names are already written in the book of life, but our names are removed from the book when we do not repentance from our sins. Through Christ, we are now not measured by the sin we commit but given grace through repentance. We all fall short but now, through Jesus, we can repent and receive God's grace.

Revelation 22:19 NIV: "And if anyone takes words away from this scroll of prophecy, God will take away from that person any share in the tree of life and in the Holy City, which are described in this scroll."

God planned to have all of us with him in Heaven. God gave us all the choice to choose him and have eternal life, and it is never too late if you are alive.

2 Peter 3:9 NIV: "The Lord is not slow in keeping his promise, as some understand slowness. Instead, he is patient with you, not wanting anyone to perish, but everyone to come to repentance."

We are all important to him because he is our father, no matter the race or belief. He wants us all back with him. Even the sins like fornication and seeking vengeance are gateways for the devil to use you to hurt God's children. As we look to judge all rapists, sex traffickers, murderers, and cheaters consider that they are only humans who allow the devil to use them. Although we may place more weight on their transgressions, God weighs all sins the same so follow the words of James 1: 19-20 NIV: "Quick to forgive and slow to anger."

That is why we cannot judge others. No sin is greater than the next, as God says. So, when we sentence murderers to death and are not saved before they die, we just gave the devil one extra soul away from God. This does not please God. It is disappointing to him because we did not learn to love and forgive like him. Man has sinned so much but cannot forgive as God forgave us. I believe we must focus on rehabilitation and not condemnation because the devil can use any of us if we are not intentional of his attacks. Sadly, those who died unsaved will never get an opportunity to go to heaven, and sadly God does not want that for his children. He does not want us to be left here to be tormented by the devil. He already defeated the devil for us. Our father needs us to use our authority to do his will on this Earth and defeat the devil's plans while we wait for Jesus' return. If we all resisted the devil, he would have to flee, as it says in James 4.

James 4:7 NIV: "Submit yourselves, then, to God. Resist the devil, and he will flee from you."

He is only here because we have not all resisted him. We must work together and pray for each other when we fall short. The devil tries to use us all in different ways so let us not try to single out people by sin but decide to redeem, love, and pray for them all. Pray for your enemies and those who do wrong because we do not know what the devil has been doing to them all their lives that led them to this moment. We do not know what they are going through. Help God redeem each soul by loving them and praying for them. Once they experience God, there will be no way for them not to fall in love with him as we did. We must learn to forgive and not condemn the criminals. They need redemption to find God, not just to be "reprimanded" and stored away for a period in solitary confinement. Rehabilitation is key, but instead, they are treated unfavorably because of the anger and judgment within man's hearts. If we treated others how we would want to be treated when we fell short, then justice would not be a goal but a bare minimum.

Ecclesiastes 7:8-9 NIV: "*The end of a matter is better than its beginning, and patience is better than pride. Do not be quickly provoked in your spirit, for anger resides in the lap of fools.*"

Having "willpower" will not be enough to fight off the devil because he is a spirit. You must use the Holy Spirit, found inside us already, to defeat him. Adam and Eve caused us to be born into sin in this world, but we are made new creatures through God through salvation.

2 Corinthians 5:17 NIV: "*Therefore, if anyone is in Christ, the new creation has come: The old has gone; the new is here!*"

All those lost souls are orphans looking for their spiritual father to fill the God-sized void that can only be filled with his love. It is our job to show them how he loves them by displaying his love to them. It will help them find their way back to him. Christianity was created for us to build a relationship with God. The Bible tells stories that God wants us to know. Therefore, it is a mixture of books written by different individuals who had an opportunity to experience God, Jesus, and/or the Holy Spirit.

I believe the devil gets the advantage when we do not forgive. It keeps us bound so that we cannot seek full purpose in God. The devil uses anything to keep us distracted—even the offenses he causes humans to do toward other humans. We stay so fixed on each other and do not realize that something is operating against both of us, and it happens to the best of us. COVID 19 was the devil's way to bring fear to society, and since that stopped working for a while, he started to use Anger. The corruption in this world is strengthening, and we are reacting wrong. The opposite of faith is fear, and if we are consumed by fear, then where does our faith in God fits in? The first tactic to get us to doubt our beliefs took away hope for some. Then the second phase was anger which would not have happened if fear were not implemented first. People were feeling hopeless from being confined at home and to TV/Social media. Then all the social injustice or topics stir up anger in people to give up their faith. We focused more on political and social issues than we did on God and what he was trying to teach us this season. We all are battling fear. I pray for the ones who are falling for the tricks of the enemy, but we should not fear because God is King. God made the Heavens and the Earth, and he has all power. God is reassuring his children in this season, and the devil is just tormenting the people more with anger and fear. God loves us because he is our father. The devil is a bully, so he only uses those who allow him to use them. Every day it seems like a different part of the book of Revelation is manifesting, so I stand in my decision to spread the word of God. His children are secured in him because only God can save us now.

Luke 6:27-28 NIV: "But to you who are listening, I say: Love your enemies, do good to those who hate you, bless those who curse you, pray for those who mistreat you."

I pity the racist supremacy groups who just allow hatred to develop in their hearts. Sadly, they probably were raised in this way of thinking all their lives and never had a chance to love without obligation. The devil made sure to plant his seeds in them when they were young, and all they wanted to do is be loved by their parents. The only way to earn that love was through the submission of their parents' beliefs. Granted, we all encounter people of all races and ethnicities that may hurt us, but the devil made it his mission to instill values in them that made their identity faulty. Whenever you act on a lie, that lie gains power in your life. They have not learned that their value is not depending on their performance. Not even having control over things or proving your worth by your net worth determines their value. Only if they could understand that, because God sent Jesus to die for their sins and the magnitude of God's love for them, they are loved. It would help them combat the devil's plan for their lives. He made sure that the impact of disappointing encounters with outside races cultivated their paranoia. Supremacy means being superior to all others in authority, power, or status, but that means you have the mindset of someone constantly living to take your spot.

The devil told the same lie to Eve, which caused her to eat the fruit. He made her think that God was holding her back from being like God. She did not understand that man was made in God's image and were heirs of God. Even though Adam and Eve were fully developed, they did not know good or evil, like children. So, this was the first planted seed of the enemy. He attacked her when she was impressionable and vulnerable, like a child. He used that against her. The devil is feeding the same lie to these supremacy groups while they are young. The devil came in the form of a serpent because that was a familiar creature in the garden of Eden. When he infected the supremacy group's minds they were young. He came in the form of their parents and relatives (familiar) when he infected them with his lies. The whole point is that Eve was a child of God, so she already was made in God's image. Kids are their parents, so she had all the power and authority she needed but she gave it all up because of a lie. When God gave me this understanding, it helped me love all his children more. That kind of paranoia/fear will develop into a level of hatred no man can deter. Only God's healing can. They were never safe to trust anyone outside of their race and had to put up walls. Paranoia is fear. That is why being kind and praying for them is the best we can do—just planting a seed of good in their lives that will grow with God's love.

Genesis 3: 1-5 NIV: "Now the serpent was more crafty than any of the wild animals the LORD God had made. He said to the woman, "Did God really say, 'You must not eat from any tree in the garden'?" The woman said to the serpent, "We may eat fruit from the trees in the garden, but God did say, 'You must not eat fruit from the tree that is in the middle of the garden, and you must not touch it, or you will die.'" "You will not certainly die," the serpent said to the woman. "For God knows that when you eat from it, your eyes will be opened, and you will be like God, knowing good and evil."

I also pity my people, the African American population, because many of them have been born with a fear of these supremacists. In some of them, it formed hatred in their hearts for a whole race. The devil attacks our minds with negativity and then attacks us physically so that he puts us through situations that make us view life as a prison. This is so that we never succeed. You must speak faith to deter what negative outcome you may experience. Remind yourself that it is only temporary because what you speak over your life does manifest if you believe it. The capacity to forgive is impactful, and without it, we stay in bondage, and God cannot fully use us. Everyone wealthy or rich is not of God. Even the devil can provide riches on Earth only. The difference is that when he offers riches, you must give your soul to him to be a slave to his cause and then experience total damnation when you die. God just wants your love. He blesses us because he loves us unconditionally. Nothing we did made us deserve his blessings (wealth and prosperity). As Christians, we choose to push the divine agenda because we want everyone to have a chance at experiencing true love without obligation. We want people to have a home in heaven and not be tormented in hell. The devil tries to portray Hell as a party, just like sex traffickers promise people financial security and support. Though they are deeply flawed, they are more deeply loved. Even when we sin, God loves us unconditionally because he measured us by the grace that he bestowed upon us when Jesus died for our sins.

Hebrews 12:15 NIV: "See to it that no one falls short of the grace of God and that no bitter root grows up to cause trouble and defile many."

Martin Luther King Jr. was right about fighting with love and peace because he understood that spiritual warfare manifests in the flesh. If we help God find his way into their hearts, then he can redeem them and get the glory. We must see that our purpose is to serve a divine plan. The plan is bigger than ours. We are doing it for the generations to come. The purpose is always meant to challenge the current version of yourself. The purpose is something that is bigger than you and pushes for evolution. We must start to live for things that impact more than just us. Change may be slow, but we must see it as something that will manifest for future generations. Therefore, those individuals who chose to march with Martin Luther King Jr were willing to risk persecution to make a difference. They took that risk for the sake of our generations.

Matthew 5:43-45 NIV: "You have heard that it was said, 'Love your neighbor and hate your enemy.' But I tell you, love your enemies and pray for those who persecute you, that you may be children of your Father in heaven. He causes his sun to rise on the evil and the good and sends rain on the righteous and the unrighteous."

People tend to underestimate the impact of their actions, and therefore boundaries are necessary. As Christians, we must learn always to speak life and love to people. We should not judge them for their shortcomings as if we never were sinners. If a person is still struggling with sin patterns, we should uplift them and provide the resources that would benefit them on their journey. People who are damaged are not beyond repair. They just have not let God fully transform their lives yet. God takes the beauty from the ashes. It is our job to discern whether someone is an assignment or a friend. An assignment from God is given to us for his will to be done on Earth. When someone is your assignment, this person can be lost or damaged and needs to experience God's love through you. We are image-bearers. If someone is your assignment, they would not be an individual you would give full access to you. This person is still learning to love the right way, and they require more grace than a person who has been renewed in Christ. This individual is learning their identity in Christ and resolving past issues and cannot commit to you, but sometimes we give too much access to a damaged person, and they hurt us. If we guard our hearts, it would be easier to give grace when they miss the mark (let us down), but instead, we experience pain or even judge them. We must know that our vulnerability (attachment) could lead to betrayal because they cannot love us properly. We must stop thinking that they can match our level of love and understand that assignments have end dates. That person was not meant to be a part of your journey, only a part of the season you are in. Be the light that God needs you to be for this person and provide them grace when they fall short. Help them to repent and progress without condemnation. Lead them back to God and be at a place where you can move on to your next season without them. Like children, we must give room for error because we understand that there is a process to learning new behaviors. Give them grace when they fall short and help them understand the severity of the problem and disciple them.

One trait I identified about myself is my capacity to love. I used to look at it as a curse, but I understand that it was a gift that God gave me to love his children on Earth wholeheartedly. My capacity to forgive and empathize was a great trait.... when used right. I had to discern from a friend and an assignment. I used to struggle in this area, and it caused me to put up a wall for everyone. As I got older, I realized that if I used my discernment, I would place a gate that allowed me to give access to the right people. If you know you have this gift, then you must nurture and understand that gift. Understand that improper use of this gift causes more damage than good. I learned how not to be careless with such a big gift because that gift helped me remain the light in this dark world. When I allowed myself to be vulnerable with the wrong people, the pain from the disappointment made me wish I could be coldhearted. It is not in my nature. Viewing my gift as a curse caused me to view God differently because I felt like he burdened me with this gift. I had to read his scriptures to understand that he gave me what he had in himself. Like most Earthly fathers who give characteristics, physical features, and blood type to their children, God gave me his heart. I found comfort in knowing that. So, I learned to guard my heart and become selective of my surroundings. Understanding the difference between a friend and an assignment. This gift is a blessing from

God, and I see its impact every day. Forgiveness helped me to heal my heart and move forward with purpose. If we begin to understand our gifts and how we are supposed to use them, then we can maximize the experiences that God wanted us to have. This would prevent the pain of mismanaged attachments and more room for grace and mercy for others. God surrounds us with the right people as we pursue purpose in him. Seek God regarding your new surroundings, and he will help you identify people's intentions. God will reveal their true character to you, be vigilant. Using our gifts as intended would cause less offense and less baggage from resentment in our lives. We will experience less hurt from people because we would know not to give access to certain people.

From Paper to Process

Choosing to Forgive. The devil tries to attack every person so he can plant a seed that would distract us from our destiny. I realized that the people who hurt me were being used by the enemy. The devil uses them to hurt me. Taking the human out of the equation, helped me to focus on the real enemy (devil). It allowed me to win the battles of spiritual warfare. Spiritual warfare does not affect me because I will rebuke the enemy and discern against his plans of attack. Spiritual warfare is when you fight against the work of evil forces, evil spirits, or demons that intervene in human affairs in various ways.

Something I learned from Pastor Mike Todd about forgiveness is that the things about us that we may hate or wish we can change did not start big. It was left unaddressed, and it festered. God says you are going to have to be intentional about forgiveness. God requires forgiveness in his covenant because he already supplied it through his covenant. Forgiveness was extended to you by God so that you can learn to give it to others. People can sin against us just like we sinned against God, and we must learn to give grace. It is hard to give forgiveness to somebody when you think you are better than them. We all need the grace of God. We all need to repent, and we all need forgiveness. We all have a predetermined level that a person can reach that we think is beyond God's forgiveness, but that is not true. When you do not forgive, you will derail your destiny, holding on to people who are not supposed to be a part of it. You will not be able to forgive them on your own. You cannot put your faith in the person; put your faith in God over the person. With wisdom comes understanding of the mindset of a broken and damaged person. We are not aware of the pain in their lives that made them into who they are. We must allow God's love to penetrate their scabs and wounds so that he may uproot the planted seeds of the enemy.

F.O.R.G.I.V.E (Face U, Own Your Part, Remind U, Grieve U, Insulate U, Value U, Embrace U)

After watching Pastor Mike Todd's sermon on forgiveness, his acronym F.O.R.G.I.V.E truly redefined my journey towards forgiveness. The process of facing yourself by forgiving yourself for the mistakes you made. We tend to blame ourselves for the wrong we experience, like allowing ourselves to get played by someone or allowing ourselves to get close to them just so that they can hurt us. Even putting yourself in a predicament that you knew was not beneficial to you—causing yourself to drink and lose control, etc. Forgive yourself! God can help you forgive those who hurt you, but you must forgive yourself before you can forgive them. It is not your fault. It is not their fault. It was the enemy's attack on your life. Next is owning your part in what transpired. Consider that God's grace is sufficient to forgive all. Then remind yourself of who God called you to be. Do not let the enemy throw guilt and shame at you. You need to remind yourself that Jesus died for your sins and God's grace redeemed us. You are chosen. The best days are yet to come for God's children, and that includes you. Failure is an event and not a person. Mistakes are a part of growing, so learn from the mistake. The next step is to grieve you. Grieve that life you thought you were going to have. Understand that you are not your mistakes. It is okay if you are not where you thought you should be in life. It is never too late to start a business, get a degree, have a family, pursue purpose, etc. Review the Lamentation book in the Bible. Get your deliverance! The devil can only win if you think he has power. He is beneath us and lives every day trying to convince us to quit. Insulate yourself with people who will support you and help you push through the process of forgiving yourself and others. Embrace yourself with love and the love of God. Allow him to cover your heart and heal it with both hands. Lay in God's arms and meditate with him. Forgiveness is freedom, and without it, we are bound and will fall victim to the enemy's attack.

Forgiveness Scriptures

Matthew 6:12-15 NIV: "And forgive us our debts, as we also have forgiven our debtors. And lead us not into temptation but deliver us from the evil one. For if you forgive other people when they sin against you, your heavenly Father will also forgive you. But if you do not forgive others their sins, your Father will not forgive your sins."

Ephesians 4:26-32 NIV: "[In your anger, do not sin]: Do not let the sun go down while you are still angry, and do not give the devil a foothold. Anyone who has been stealing must steal no longer but must work, doing something useful with their own hands, that they may have something to share with those in need. Do not let any unwholesome talk come out of your mouths, but only what is helpful for building others up according to their needs, that it may benefit those who listen. And do not grieve the Holy Spirit of God, with whom you were sealed for the day of redemption. Get rid of all bitterness, rage and anger, brawling, and slander, along with every form of malice. Be kind and compassionate to one another, forgiving each other, just as in Christ God forgave you.

Luke 17:1-10 NIV: "Jesus said to his disciples: 'Things that cause people to stumble are bound to come, but woe to anyone through whom they come. It would be better for them to be thrown into the sea with a millstone tied around their neck than to cause one of these little ones to stumble. So, watch yourselves.' 'If your brother or sister sins against you, rebuke them, and if they repent, forgive them. Even if they sin against you seven times in a day and seven times come back to you saying, 'I repent,' you must forgive them.' The apostles said to the Lord, 'Increase our faith!' He replied, 'If you have faith as small as a mustard seed, you can say to this mulberry tree, [Be uprooted and planted in the sea] and it will obey you.' Suppose one of you has a servant plowing or looking after the sheep. Will he say to the servant when he comes in from the field, 'Come along now and sit down to eat'? Won't he rather say, 'Prepare my supper, get yourself ready and wait on me while I eat and drink; after that, you may eat and drink'? Will he thank the servant because he did what he was told to do? So, you also, when you have done everything you were told to do, should say, 'We are unworthy servants; we have only done our duty."

Matthew 18:21-35 NIV: Then Peter came to Jesus and asked, "Lord, how many times shall I forgive my brother or sister who sins against me? Up to seven times? Jesus answered, "I tell you, not seven times, but seventy-seven times. "Therefore, the kingdom of heaven is like a king who wanted to settle accounts with his servants. As he began the settlement, a man who owed him ten thousand bags of gold was brought to him. Since he was not able to pay, the master ordered that he and his wife and his children and all that he had be sold to repay the debt. "At this, the servant fell on his knees before him. 'Be patient with me,' he begged, 'and I will pay back everything.' The servant's master took pity on him, canceled the debt, and let him go. "But when that servant went out, he found one of his fellow servants who owed him a hundred silver coins. He grabbed him and began to choke him. 'Pay back what you owe me!' he demanded. "His fellow servant fell to his knees and begged him, 'Be patient with me, and I will pay it back.' "But he refused. Instead, he went off and had the man thrown into prison until he could pay the debt. When the other servants saw what had happened, they were outraged and went and told their master everything that had happened. "Then the master called the servant in. 'You wicked servant,' he said, 'I canceled all that debt of yours because you begged me to. Shouldn't you have had mercy on your fellow servant just as I *had on you?' In anger, his master handed him over to the jailers to be tortured until he should pay back all he owed. "This is how my heavenly Father will treat each of you unless you forgive your brother or sister from your heart."*

Roman 8:28-29 NIV: "And we know that in all things God works for the good of those who love him, who have been called according to his purpose. For those God foreknew he also predestined to be conformed to the image of his Son, that he might be the firstborn among many brothers and sisters.

5

SIN, GOD'S GRACE & OUR BIRTHRIGHT

The purpose of sin is to allow the devil to use/access us in the flesh. After Adam and Eve ate the apple, they began to know good and evil, which planted the seed of sin in all humankind. Sin is a gateway for the devil to use us. If we repent, after we have sinned, we close that door so the devil cannot use us. Even if we may fall short and commit the sin again, always REPENT and make provisions to improve. The flesh is weak; the spirit is strong. If we took the time to understand that we all fall short, then we would not judge. Sexual impurity is a gateway sin to being used by the devil because we make our flesh primary, and it is flawed. Insecurities also provide access for the devil to use us because they can manifest into jealousy, paranoia, fear, infidelity, etc. The devil uses these traits to make us act out of character, which can sometimes cause pain to others or cause pain to our purpose and future.

We sometimes wonder why God would cause us to have these weaknesses. Consider this… after we left the garden of Eden, the seed of sin was planted in us by the devil. When Jesus died for our sins, he left us the Holy Spirit, which would help us overpower the sinful urges of the flesh. Most of the time, it was exposed to us at a young age by the devil, and it lay dormant until we got older. For some, it manifested into different traits that we struggle to manage or suppress daily. I experienced Lust at a young age, being exposed to homosexuality, pornography, and masturbation. Some would think I would have no chance to be sanctified but that is not true. Acknowledging that my urges were wrong and that I was exposed to them helped me ask God for help in resolving them. Growing in my faith and learning more about my authority and the Holy Spirit, given to me by God, I overcame my iniquities and untrained my mind of all that I was exposed to. Understanding that God loves me and forgave me of my sins made it easier.

Isaiah 43:25 NIV: "I, even I, am he who blots out your transgressions, for my own sake, and remembers your sins no more."

Hebrews 8:12 NIV: "For I will forgive their wickedness and will remember their sins no more."

Micah 7:18-19 NIV: "Who is a God like you, who pardons sin and forgives the transgression of the remnant of his inheritance? You do not stay angry forever but delight to show mercy. You will again have compassion on us; you will tread our sins underfoot and hurl all our iniquities into the depths of the sea."

As I stay in God's word, the devil cannot find opportunities to make me sin and open that gateway for him to use me. I remain in God's word because it is a safe place and assurance that the Holy Spirit, in me, is greater than my flesh. I pray to God every day, "As I decrease, Lord, I pray you to increase in me." Keeping my spirit right is what should matter because Earth is not forever. This world is not ours. Jesus will return, and after the final coming, there will only be Heaven and Hell. I believe Earth was created as a neutral ground after Adam and Eve were banished from Eden. Once Jesus makes his final returns for his children, Earth will no longer be necessary/neutral. Hell will come upon Earth, and all the remaining inhabitants would succumb to the wrath of the devil.

When Jesus died, he left the Holy Spirit within us, so we have the authority to rebuke the devil. The devil is a Spirit, so when we try to use our willpower (flesh) to combat him, it does not work. Therefore, we fall short because we are not fighting fire with fire. We need to use our spiritual (Holy Spirit within us) to overcome him. We tap into our inherited power by reading the word of God because he teaches us how to use it. He reminds us that we are worthy and have authority on this Earth, but we must believe it. My spirit helps me combat the devil because I use the authority God has given me to rebuke him.

James 4:7 NIV: "Submit yourselves, then, to God. Resist the devil, and he will flee from you."

John 14:15-31 NIV: "If you love me, keep my commands. And I will ask the Father, and he will give you another advocate to help you and be with you forever— the Spirit of truth. The world cannot accept him because it neither sees him nor knows him. But you know him, for he lives with you and will be in you. I will not leave you as orphans; I will come to you. Before long, the world will not see me anymore, but you will see me. Because I live, you also will live. On that day, you will realize that I am in my Father, and you are in me, and I am in you. Whoever has my commands and keeps them is the one who loves me. The one who loves me will be loved by my Father, and I too will love them and show myself to them."

Then Judas (not Judas Iscariot) said, "But, Lord, why do you intend to show yourself to us and not to the world?" Jesus replied, "Anyone who loves me will obey my teaching. My Father will love them, and we will come to them and make our home with them. Anyone who does not love me will not obey my teaching. These words you hear are not my own; they belong to the Father who sent me.' All this I have spoken while still with you. 26 But the Advocate, the Holy Spirit, whom the Father will send in my name, will teach you all things and will remind you of everything I have said to you. Peace I leave with you; my peace I give you. I do not give to you as the world gives. Do not let your hearts be troubled, and do not be afraid.

"You heard me say, 'I am going away, and I am coming back to you.' If you loved me, you would be glad that I am going to the Father, for the Father is greater than I. I have told you now before it happens so that when it does happen, you will believe. I will not say much more to you, for the prince of this world is coming. He has no hold over me, but he comes so that the world may learn that I love the Father and do exactly what my Father has commanded me. Come now; let us leave."

From Paper to Process:

While I grew in my faith in God, I used to find it intimidating when Christians used to say, "oh, I hear from God" or "God directs me." I used to think it was a certain voice I should listen out for, but it was not that all the time for me. It was more of thoughts that would come to me or ideas I would not have ever thought about on my own. People always called me an "old soul" because I was always full of wisdom and understanding for my age. I realized this was the case because my gift was ministry, and the Holy Spirit would give me the wisdom to give to other people that I honestly did not know where it came from. I even had a harder time reiterating it. That was my way of knowing those words were of God and not of me. I allowed God to use me as a source for wisdom sharing.

Some people may feel like it is impossible to get to that level, but it just takes time. As we experience more quiet time with God, we will begin to learn his voice, and through the reading of his word. Just give it time. If you want to learn a new skill, you take the time to study and adapt it to everyday practice. The same practice is required if you want to start to hear from God. All you must do is invest more time into his word and more quiet time/ meditation with him, and you will be able to filter his voice from the voices of the enemy. What I like to tell people is that compartmentalizing God in your life only does you a disservice. God is the "all and all." If you want to bear good fruit in all aspects of your life, then you must let him lead you towards good soil. To grow in your faith and understanding of God, you must understand how powerful he is. Believe that he can change ANY SITUATION in your life, not just finances or relationships.

Growing by faith exercises will not benefit someone who is trying to classify God. It works for someone who understands that God is "all in all," and they want to include him in every decision of their lives. Not just when it comes to certain aspects of their lives. I never get nervous anymore when obstacles arise because I know the God I serve and that my big problems are molecular compared to my God. I serve a Big God! Faith will only work if you truly believe that God is Almighty and that he gives you authority on this Earth. To gain an understanding of this, you must know how much power God has. You must understand his credentials. Like when someone obtains a degree from a college/ university: The university's credentials give them the power to deem you qualified and highly capable of fulfilling the skills required in your desired profession (degree). When they issue you a degree, this is the authority they give you to make impactful decisions in your profession. You must know that you have authority from God, who is the almighty, and that you are joint-heirs with Christ. Anything short of this understanding will keep you from believing that you have the authority that God has given you.

James 1:12-15 NIV: "Blessed is the one who perseveres under trial because, having stood the test, that person will receive the crown of life that the Lord has promised to those who love him. When tempted, no one should say, 'God is tempting me.' For God cannot be tempted by evil, nor does he tempt anyone, but each person is tempted when they are dragged away by their own evil desire and enticed. Then, after desire has conceived, it gives birth to sin; and sin, when it is full-grown, gives birth to death."

6

WE ARE IMAGE BEARERS & OVERCOMERS

God's calling on your life is bigger than any crisis that arises. Remember to push through the pain because weeping may tarry for the night, but joy comes with the morning - "Psalm 30:1-5 ESV." We do not appreciate the good without knowing what bad is like. Be grateful and know he has you. Pray for the children without parents, and God will protect them. God gives us authority on this Earth. Until we know who we are and the amount of power we have over our lives, the enemy works every day to make us think that we do not have control. We are joint-heirs with Jesus Christ and have authority on this Earth through the Holy Spirit. The Holy Spirit is already in us; we just need to cultivate it. Make your testimony your tool to help save lives from the hands of the enemy.

Know that there is no situation on this Earth bigger than God. Through him, anything you face, God will help you endure with peace. Even when bad news comes your way, remember who your God is. Remind yourself that you serve a Big God. If your faith begins to waver, always surround yourself with people that remind you of who you are and who God is. Always remember what he has gotten you through in the past and remind yourself of his promises. Getting through adversity requires a mindset adjustment. Continue to believe in him even during the trial. As you go through your trials, find scriptures that relate to your struggle, and as you pray, remind God of his word and his promises to you through scripture.

Matthew 5:16 NIV: "In the same way, let your light shine before others, that they may see your good deeds and glorify your Father in heaven."

Our job, as Christians, is to be Image bearers of God. We are supposed to display his love, mercy, grace, and forgiveness on this Earth. Our jobs are not to condemn people. We are supposed to help those who are lost. We never know a person's past, so do not be quick to judge their present. I am saved, and I do my best not to sin. I am celibate, and I do my best every day to do right by God. Some may not be pursuing God like I am, and that is fine. Our job is not to force religion on people. It is to show God through us and let God redeem his lost children. We minister God's word to everyone. We show love and mercy to them and let God reveal himself to them in due time. Everyone will have their trials, tribulations, and testimonies. It is good to give advice, but it is not to judge or force people into Christianity. If a non-believer did not ask you to be their accountability partner, please do not take on the role. We need to focus on seeking God for ourselves and not worrying about people's business. If you are concerned about others people's lifestyles please plan to dedicate your life to helping them and counseling, which most people who judge would not. If you think your role is to condemn and banish people out of the kingdom of God, you are sadly mistaken. The kingdom of God is not ours to reign. GOD GAVE US ALL GRACE. Everyone has sinned, so GOD says he weighs every sin the same. Confess your sins to one another and pray for each other.

James 5:16 NIV: "Therefore, confess your sins to each other and pray for each other so that you may be healed. The prayer of a righteous person is powerful and effective."

Proverbs 24:16-18 NIV: "for though the righteous fall seven times, they rise again, but the wicked stumble when calamity strikes. Do not gloat when your enemy falls; when they stumble, do not let your heart rejoice, or the Lord will see and disapprove and turn his wrath away from them.

D.E.S.T.I.N.Y (Dreams, Environment, Subconscious, Time, Inspiration, Network, You)

God does not just give us provisions and gifts to complete an assignment and not give us power and resources. We first must write the vision down and make it plain and allow his will to be done. If God gives you an assignment, he is going to help you do it. Time waits for no man. When God gives you an assignment that can provide you wealth, and his name the glory, you must act on it. You may think you have time, but God does not need to give you a second chance. What you will not do, someone else will. God is on a mission to restore all his children to him so that the devil does not win. God has a plan that requires us to play our roles to combat the tactics of the enemy. If God waits on you to get it together, then lives can be jeopardized. When we pursue purpose, it is for a divine plan that is bigger than us. God is not in the business of missing out on saving a soul to wait on us to figure out if we should pursue purpose or not. God gives us gifts to monetize it and not lack, but we first need to change our mindsets. No more victimization or poverty mindsets. We must think of strategy and go into prayer with God to gain provision. Do not let the enemy attach that wasteful spirit to you. Do not stay stagnant and waste time. If you have an idea, do it and do it scare because the faith of a mustard seed is all you need. Things will not just drop on your lap or into your life. You must push forward and watch God elevate you.

God is making ways in this season, and he needs us to step into our predestined roles. God has given us all gifts, and it is our time to monetize them. God gave you those same gifts to help you prosper on this Earth as it is in Heaven. If you have a goal, then figure it out with God, and he will provide witty ideas. Ask me how I came up with C.R.E.A.M. I plan to pour out my knowledge to others because I love God's children and need everyone to understand the magnitude of their gifts. Use the gifts God gave you. Your gifts are yours regardless of repentance, but with repentance and obedience, God's anointing catapults everything.

Live for today because you never know when it is your time. Someone can die when they are 30 years old, and someone can live to see 100 years old. Since you do not know when your time is up, do not think that there is no reason to pursue your purpose because you are older. Start your life over and make provisions because it is never too late if you are alive. It is never too late because you never know when your time is up. Only God tells you your time is up and not a moment sooner. Start that business plan, cultivate the ideas, pursue things that you have always wanted to pursue, and make provisions in your life that give you a better relationship with your spouse, family member, or friend. Your purpose on this Earth is not yet completed, and that is why you are still here, so continue to push forward and do the work of the Lord. Do not limit yourself because God is limitless. Write down the vision and make it plain. Seek his counsel on it, and he will give you the tools and the ideas necessary for your plan to take root and flourish. There is no timeline on when success begins for someone, but it does require obedience and discipline. God wants us all to do great things because we reflect on him. He wants us to be wealthy so that people can see the fruits of our labor, but we must get to work! You must know what to do with what God has blessed you with. He does not want to give you something that will sabotage you. He only wants to give you things that will elevate you, so consult him with your visions. Let him help you cultivate your dreams. Always remember that the closer you get to your purpose, the devil will throw any and everything your way to try to knock you off your mission. If he does not distract you, then he will try to destroy you. Stay focused on the bigger picture as no weapon formed against you shall prosper. If the enemy is not attacking, then you are doing something wrong.

Everything I say is because I love God's children (lost and found). We must start living our lives for God and not for man. What people say about us or what we say about others does not matter. We must start focusing on our personal growth and development and not what society wants us to focus on. It just makes us forget Who We are and makes us focus on what other people are doing. That is not what God wanted us to do. He wanted us to love each other, grow with each other and help each other thrive. Not to bash each other but to help each other understand who we are in Christ. There is no limit to who we can be on this Earth. The difference is what we choose to make of ourselves.

7

SOCIETY'S DEPICTION OF GOD

There are things in life God wants us to experience to help prepare us for the role he wants us to play in society. Every trial or experience God gives us is to build character and increase our wisdom. However, some people believe that all experiences are God's doing. The devil walks around on Earth trying to distract us from our purpose. He places events or people in our path to complete his mission. The devil comes to attack us and leave us with wounds and memories that leave a hole in our souls that only God can restore. The devil tries to bring people into our life as distractions all the time. God tries to inform us that it is not part of his plan. God is a gentleman. If you do not want to do his will, then he will not force us to. When God advises us not to pursue those types of experiences and we still do, we assume God wanted us to go through that experience. This is incorrect. God prefers us and even advises us not to. Nonetheless, we choose to go through the experience. He let us go through it, and he uses everything bad/good for our good in the end. All your mistakes and all your shortcomings, he used them to benefit you regardless. But make no mistake: if it is his choice, he would have preferred you not to experience them because that was not his design for your life.

Romans 8:28 NIV: "And we know that in all things God works for the good of those who love him, who have been called according to his purpose."

Analogy time: If your parents allowed you to go to a party and then at this party you get drunk, do drugs, and get taken advantage of, is this your parents' fault? You are upset with your parents as though it was their fault that you experience it. They would not let you go through that. They did not want you to experience that but you never called your parents to say, "Hey, I am going to do drugs and get drunk. Is that okay?" Your parents would have said, "no, come home." How would they know if you did not tell them? They would not have let you out ever again. They originally believed that they taught you all the values and wisdom you would need to make sound decisions without them but this is not the case. Subsequently, if you chose to make bad decisions without them knowing, how can they help you? If they knew what transpired, they would have realized that there are things they need to continue teaching you about how to conduct yourself in public. Some people may argue that "if God sees all, why does he not tell us not to do it or stop it?" My response is…. if you cannot hear God tell you no because you do not spend time with God to learn his voice, how would you know when he tells you not to do something?

The devil is a spirit. The Holy Spirit is a spirit, so if they all operate in the spiritual realm, they both have access to talking with you in your mind. If you choose not to understand that the devil sometimes encourages poor decisions, sin, and discourages us in your mind, you will have a hard time battling him. The devil does these things easily if you do not build up your spirit to be stronger than your flesh. Your flesh lacks self-control and will fall short, so you must take that time and build up the spirit within you to learn God's voice and make better decisions. This is crucial so that you know when situations like this happen, the devil's telling you "yeah, go ahead," and then God's telling you "no," and you will know the difference. However, through the reading of God's word, getting drunk and high is a sin. I am not judging just making an observation. Some situations are avoidable if we choose to understand why God made it a sin. It was made sin as protection. Being impaired leaves room for the devil to send obstacles your way. It also was to let you know that you will decipher what good behavior is and what bad behavior is if you invest the time in his word as God gives us free will 100% of the time. He is not going to make you do something different. He gives you Free will. He also gives guidance to whoever chooses him and heeds his voice. He does not impose his advice on you without your consent. God is a gentleman, so unless you let him lead, then he will not come in. He allows us to live our lives. If you choose to follow his provision, show his love and honor as a father, then he will do as such and advised you. God has intended a path for us already from birth to become who we are supposed to become in him. If you ask him, he will lead you where he needs you to be and give you fruitful experiences. These experiences will help cultivate you into the person he needs to fulfill your true purpose. If you choose to stray away from the path that he has then you will expose yourself more to the devil's attacks. Understand it was not God's plan. You can come back to him, and he will still use that experience for your good in the end. However, he would have preferred you not to experience it. He gives us free will at the end of the day, and he will always forgive us once we repent. When we are ready, he will help us continue the path that he had intended for us. It may seem like our path has many struggles, but some of them are attacks from the enemy. If we just chose to stick with what God had planned, we would only need to know the experiences that God needed us to have.

Nonetheless, our testimonies help other people learn from our mistakes and how we overcame them with God's help. It also tells them how not to pursue those things. If we just stick to the path that God has for us, our lives would be a lot simpler versus trying to figure it out on our own. I used to think I knew what was best for me and that God does not. Then I found out that I do not know, at all, what was best for me. Testimonies help inform people that they can overcome anything with God, even things we cause.

Once God delivers you from your mistakes, it is best to ask for wisdom so that we do not make the same mistakes. Following God is a choice that you would have to make. To heed his advice is a choice. Suppose you want to live your life without God's provision; that is your choice. However, we must stop blaming God for things that happen to us on our journey without him. God gives us grace, so he does not punish us. The devil does all that by himself. Someone choosing God's provision understands the glory and peace that comes with knowing you are secure in any situation. I feel more secure and fulfilled being renewed in Christ than while I was lost in this world. This world has a way of extracting all the Hope out of you when you do not have faith in God. Knowing there is a God gives me hope for a better tomorrow.

8

GOD, THROUGH THE EYES OF THE BEHOLDER

As America is big on sports, I would like to make this analogy to spark some thought for my readers. God is a Coach, and we are Teammates. We gain individual growth and self-awareness during practice (Our alone time with God or in God's word). We learn our weaknesses and who we are as we turn those weaknesses into strengths. During the Game (in the world), as we pursue purpose and do God's will on Earth (as image-bearers of Christ) we use teamwork to fulfill the work of the Lord on Earth. We work together to win (save lives, help all rediscover God and their true identities in him). The key thing to this is that no one can do your part but you. Your purpose is tailored to you. God needs us all to fulfill our calling to work in unison to win the game called salvation.

God is the Spiritual Father that we would view as an ideal parent, but we all did not get the opportunity to have the ideal parents in this life. Sometimes that stems from our parents not getting the opportunity to be raised by the ideal parents as well. As you can see, it is a generational disparity, and some tend to base their spiritual father on the character of their Earthly father. We should not. God is not a man who should lie nor a son of man that he should repent because he is all-knowing and righteous. He does not get tempted or can be used by the devil-like our Earthly fathers can. He loves us despite who we are and what we do. Instead of judging and placing blame, let us make the choice today not to be our parents. Let us stop the cycle of generational curses. Let us get out of the victim role and get into the victor role because that means you have overcome adversity.

If your family owns a business, then they plan for you to one day take over that business. They tend to dedicate most of your formative years to grooming you for that role. God does the same things with us. When you were born, God knew the final plan he had for your life. So, when you go to God and ask him to use you, he will begin grooming you to be the person he needs you to become to fulfill your destiny. We all have a role in saving God's children who are lost or struggling and even those who are found. We are all human and need help, accountability, and prayer to keep us righteous. If God begins to groom you and there are traits that he needs you to unlearn or restrict you, it is for your protection. The experience could have led to pain, or it would cause you to lose some characteristics traits that you had that made you special and equipped for the purpose God had for you. He knows what experiences we will need and those we can avoid.

Trust him to know what is best for you as he created you and knows what he placed in you. He knows what would make you happy, sad, fulfilled, etc. So, give him a try and spend time with him so he can remind you who you are and guide you. Always include him in your decisions, and he will never lead you somewhere you did not need to go. Adversity builds character so expect some challenges. Just expect to learn something valuable from that challenge. Somethings we must learn before becoming that person God needs us to be to position us for greatness. This world is big, and everyone has a role to play. Teamwork is key because it takes us all to resist the devil so he truly can flee from us on the Earth. God gives us free will to decide whether we want what he has for us or to have our own life. Either you want the answer key, or you want to guess the answer; that is the difference. God's way is best because he will always have your best interest at heart and knows what you can achieve with him by your side. Your testimony would be the thing that could save someone from death or years of misery.

Our ways are not his ways.

When God tells us not to do something and we still choose to do it anyway, it is not God who punishes us because we choose not to listen to him. I want to use this analogy because I felt it was very popular when I was growing up. When your parents tell you not to put your hand on the hot stove, you touch it anyway and get burned. When your parents tell you not to put your hand on the hot stove, it protects you from getting burned. However, if you choose to put your hand on that hot stove and get burned, you cannot blame your parents. You can assume your parent was punishing you when they intended to prevent unnecessary pain. They wanted to prevent you from experiencing that pain that they did not plan for you to experience. When you go through something after God tells you not to do it, do not assume it is his way of punishing you. He gives you free will. This is his way of letting you go through what you wanted to experience versus getting protection from him. His protection causes you not to experience it. As God gave us an authority on this Earth, he also gave us free will so he will not force us not to do something. He would advise us against it, and in the end, we would have to have enough faith in him to believe what he is advising is potent. If we choose to do what we want to do, then do not wonder why it goes wrong, and please do not blame God as though he is punishing us.

God does not punish us when we choose not to listen to him. It is equivalent to a child asking to move out of their parent's house, and the parent allows them to leave. The child makes mistakes in the real world because they are not ready to handle all the things that come with adulthood. It is recommended that the child moves back home. It is the same thing when we choose to operate without God's provisions. Since we are fleshly being and spiritually immature, we tend to make mistakes. The devil will use our ignorance to attack us and leave scars that were not meant to happen. Not having that deep connection with God makes it harder to hear his warnings. We would hear his voice when he advises us when a person who enters our life is not of him. The enemy will only bring us harm, and he brings distractions. If we choose to make a bad decision that could cost us everything, we cannot blame God. Especially if we told God that we did not need him. To ignore God will only allow for the devil to sneak in to attack you. There is good and evil in this world. We associate it with humans and do not understand it is a spirit operating in the human. God cannot warn us if we choose to ignore him and think we can go through life without him. God is a gentleman, so he allowed us to experience life without him if that is what we choose. However, do not blame him for the attacks that happened to you. God does no evil. He provides grace to all of us. But just like that child who comes back home and prefers to be under their parents' roof, we return to God. After we experience the world and how meaningless it feels, we build a relationship with him and seek spiritual maturity to begin to make better decisions for our lives with his provisions.

As Jesus died for us to have grace and mercy in God's eyes, that was God giving us the upper as his protection against whatever was planning to occur. If you choose not to take heed of his words, understand you agree to whatever happens next. It is not of God's will for you. God's will would have been done with the provision he provides. I had to learn this the hard way through my past relationships and decisions that led me to unfavorable outcomes. When people say you must sacrifice to follow God, the sacrifice would not have happened if we did not pursue people or things that were not God's will for us. We cannot just expect him to bless our chaos. He wants to give us a fresh start which requires letting go of the things that bind us. I had that issue this year in my previous relationship, but it took a level of faith that I did not know I had. I had to become single and roommate with friends and let go of worldly things that I idealized. In return, God gave me a promotion; he gave me the perspective and courage to write the book, start the business, move out on my own again, and provide me with furniture at little or no cost to me. He gave me some used but good condition (normal wear and tear) furniture. I was able to design and make my own with the ideas he gave me. I began to realize what he was trying to show me: God can renew even things that are used/broken/damaged. So, for all who think you must be saved or not stuck in a sin pattern before coming to him, know that he wants you just as you are. He will help you repair the pieces. He will surround you with angels who will remind you of his love, his grace, and of the person you are becoming in Christ. Their testimonies will help ignite your faith in him and, in turn, produce your testimony for the next lost soul.

Crazy Faith

God yearns for Crazy Faith belief from his children. He loves us all, but for us to understand the true power and authority we have on this Earth, we cannot be on the fence about who we are and who God is. We cannot just tap our feet in the water to test it. God wants us to be willing to bungee jump off and believe that he will catch us. For instance, when someone goes bungee jumping, they know that they are safe and securely strapped in. They know they will make it to the other side, but everything in them will not let them jump. Sometimes, that is the same type of experience we have as believers. Sometimes we want the miracle, but we do not believe that the miracle will truly come or that we deserve it. We do not work fast for it, praise him in advance and speak it into existence. We just want God's miracle to fall on our laps. Although he does miracles, it is based on those who believe that he can make miracles happen and for non-believers to experience God. You must believe that it is possible like it says in Mark. God has faith too. He sacrificed his only son for humanity because he believed that all his children would return to him one day. He took a chance on us, so we must take a chance on him. Through all the things he has gotten us through, I know he is good for it.

Mark 11: 25 – 26 NIV: "And when you stand praying, if you hold anything against anyone, forgive them, so that your Father in heaven may forgive you your sins."

Just like the woman with the issue of blood in Mark and the Centurion's servant who believed Jesus could heal his servant just by speaking a word in Matthew:

Mark 5:25–34 NIV: "And a woman was there who had been subject to bleeding for twelve years. She had suffered a great deal under the care of many doctors and had spent all she had, yet instead of getting better, she grew worse. When she heard about Jesus, she came up behind him in the crowd and touched his cloak because she thought, 'If I just touch his clothes, I will be healed.' Immediately her bleeding stopped, and she felt in her body that she was freed from her suffering. At once, Jesus realized that power had gone out from him. He turned around in the crowd and asked, 'Who touched my clothes?' 'You see the people crowding against you,' his disciples answered, 'and yet you can ask, 'Who touched me?'' But Jesus kept looking around to see who had done it. Then the woman, knowing what had happened to her, came and fell at his feet and, trembling with fear, told him the whole truth. He said to her, "Daughter, your faith has healed you. Go in peace and be freed from your suffering."

Matthew 8: 5-13 NIV: "When Jesus had entered Capernaum, a centurion came to him, asking for help. 'Lord,' he said, 'my servant lies at home paralyzed, suffering terribly.' Jesus said to him, 'Shall I come and heal him?' The centurion replied, "Lord, I do not deserve to have you come under my roof. But just say the word, and my servant will be healed. For I, myself, am a man under authority, with soldiers under me. I tell this one, 'Go,' and he goes; and that one, 'Come,' and he comes. I say to my servant, 'Do this,' and he does it.'

When Jesus heard this, he was amazed and said to those following him, 'Truly I tell you, I have not found anyone in Israel with such great faith. I say to you that many will come from the east and the west and will take their places at the feast with Abraham, Isaac, and Jacob in the kingdom of heaven. But the subjects of the kingdom will be thrown outside, into the darkness, where there will be weeping and gnashing of teeth.' Then Jesus said to the centurion, 'Go! Let it be done just as you believed it would.' And his servant was healed at that moment."

The Centurion's type of faith impressed Jesus so much, and he said to the centurion that his servant was healed because he believed Jesus could do it. That is the faith God wants us to have in him. With this level of faith, we can heal the sick, defeat the enemy, change situations in our lives, etc. God gives us authority on this Earth and wants us to use it by declaring and decreeing over our lives. Our Father has all power, and as his heirs, we have power. Declaring that our situation is not set in stone and that God wants us to prosper, makes a difference. Do not think life is filled with sorrow, misery, and hopelessness because he will turn everything around for our good, but you must believe that he can do divine miracles. We must believe that God can do all things on this Earth and not just the small things like finding you a good parking spot or paying the bills for that month. Believe in Him for the impossible because he has power over everything on this Earth. Through your praise and perseverance, God will continuously make miracles happen on your behalf. He fights for you, so all you must do is be still, praise him, and believe in him as it says in Exodus.

Exodus 14:14 NIV: "The Lord will fight for you; you need only to be still."

The Waiting Period

Be patient. Your time is coming. I know we have this mindset that we want to do everything right away, and the waiting period does not feel great, but it is necessary. We want to get everything done right now, but sometimes God needs us to stay in the season of waiting to learn all the knowledge and character traits required to fulfill the purpose he has in store. This is necessary so that we would have all we need to teach and heal the world when we are in positions that impact lives. I love to indulge in God's word and various sermons. At any given moment, I could be talking to someone, and I would recall God's word that I would resonate with that person. Experiencing someone getting a revelation through the Holy Spirit, in me, is so fulfilling. Now I can provide people with the proper literature and structure to help them through life's challenges. When someone calls me, I now get in the habit of providing them with God's Love, some laughter, God's word, and talking about the future.

I believe faith, obedience, and repentance are what is required for God's miracles and blessings. Sometimes before God does the miraculous in your lives, he must first train us to know him and his word. Like if you wanted him to wipe away your debt, he will first teach you how to steward your finances and become financially literate. Once you embrace that process, he gives you the miracle so that you do not relapse. How can he get the glory, and you give the testimony if you go back into debt? Suppose you seek a promotion or elevate in your life. In that case, you must embrace the pressing season that leads to a renewal of your mind and surroundings that will allow you to manage the blessing or promotion, effectively. If our mindset stays stagnant, elevation will lead to our downfall and be viewed as a curse. Just like the gifts, God gives us; they will cause you more harm than good if it is mismanaged. We must learn from our mistakes and make provisions for prosperity. He is our father, and he wants to make us self-efficient on Earth because the devil will try to attack us. He does not want us to fall back into the same patterns that he redeemed us from. When you go for a loan/credit, they want to see that you do not need the loan before giving you one. A bad credit score reflects bad spending habits. Some people know better but choose not to do better. They will not give you a loan/credit with your bad habits and credit. You must repair your credit and adopt better spending habits. Once you show them good habits and a better credit score, they would give you the loan or credit. We have the answers, but we do not take the time to look for them. The Bible is a dictionary for all we need to live a righteous life and prosper.

2 Peter 1:3 NIV: *"His divine power has given us everything we need for a godly life through our knowledge of him who called us by his own glory and goodness."*

Sometimes God holds back from us because he needs us to change our priorities. Seek first the kingdom of God. This means aligning your hearts with God's will to pursue purpose. Live for a cause that is bigger than just your desire for nice things. Those nice things will be left on Earth when you die. Putting value in them will just leave a void. Would it not be more fulfilling to save a life from pain? If your answer is no, I recommend spending time with God because there is hurt and unforgiveness in your heart. I am not judging, just an observation. As children, we are taught to hate but are born with love—our capability to love changes as we experience hurt and pain because that is the devil's goal. Forgiveness is what frees us from pain, not revenge. God can trust you with his resources with a renewed heart and mind because he knows that you are trying to be a reservoir and not a dam. You will truly be after God's own heart. If he blesses you with millions, will you allow God to use it to bless the world, or will you think the blessing is for yourself? God blessed Solomon with wisdom and all the riches because he came before God and asked for the power of discernment so that he could lead God's people to live Holy. God favored him in his ability to request a selfless blessing, and God blessed him with everything (wealth and wisdom).

God wants to bless you in more ways than you can understand, but before he can do that, he must ensure that your heart is in the right place. You cannot deceive God. You must understand that with great success and influence, there are more attacks from the enemy. He must prepare you and help you work through your issues for you to stand strong during Adversity.

Matthew 5:11-12 NIV: "Blessed are you when people insult you, persecute you and falsely say all kinds of evil against you because of me. Rejoice and be glad because great is your reward in heaven, for, in the same way, they persecuted the prophets who were before you."

From Paper to Process

When I was having issues with my faith, I started to watch sermons that build my faith. During my unemployment, I felt lost and uncertain, and then I watched the Crazy Faith series by Michael Todd, and I let God lead. This helped me realize that God qualifies me for whatever position he puts me in. I had first to reprogram how I see God. I just had to trust in his will for my life and remember I am a blessing to anyone or any company. I am a quick study and problem solver, which is what God blessed me with to succeed in any role. Nothing can stop him. He is higher than all things on this Earth. If you let him, he will surround you with the right people who will bless your life in many ways but that will require getting rid of the toxic friends from you. If you are hardheaded, it was not easy for him to get rid of them like I was. I went through a season of pruning. It required me to see people's true colors and allow betrayal to rear its ugly head. God was trying to get me aligned for the purpose he has for me. Even sometimes, I would not like it, I realize it is necessary. I also experienced a season of forgiveness. Our soul holds on to all our experiences, and sometimes those experiences hold us hostage from progression. We must learn it is about quality and not quantity with friends. Before we make a new friend or partner, we have to ask God: "Is this person worth creating memories with?" He will tell you or show you who they are, and then from there, we can prevent unnecessary pain. God takes us through experiences that are necessary to build character in us, but we also create our problems when we do not consult with him before deciding. I am guilty of this, but I am progressing. I went through a very transformative 2020, and I would never regret it. It was the BEST decision I made in my life by choosing God's plan for my life and not my own.

Faith: complete trust or confidence in someone or something. I am aiming for this level of faith in God every day. I am not perfect, but I am progressing. Whatever you feel you lack, do some research, and make provisions to make it a skill. You are smart, beautiful, and powerful. You can truly do whatever you put your mind to. God had to show me that I can accomplish anything because God has my back even when I am scared or nervous about something. If he said I could do it, then I am going to do it scared. Fear is false evidence appearing real. Do it scare! You will begin to see it is just in your head; the enemy planted the spirit of discouragement. We could just be experiencing the "imposter syndrome." This makes us believe we are not capable, but we are. Through Christ and the Holy Spirit within us, we can accomplish anything.

9

THE DIVINE UNION

When we enter relationships with individuals who cannot love us, we give ourselves a God-size task that gives us a God-sized headache and heartache. We must understand we cannot change them; only God can. If a relationship started in sin, then it does not honor God. If God brought that person into your life to be a friend, support, or resource, he would not expect you to pursue fornication in a relationship and assume it is of his will. The devil also sends distractions, so be careful of who you date. If a relationship were of God's will, then premarital sex would not be something that would be pursued in the relationship because it would not honor God. However, repentance is possible because God is a restorer and a redeemer. But you still must ask yourself, "Are they the one (soul mate)?" When God finds you a partner, they would be called a soul mate. That means they are meant to grow with you and evolve with you and your divine assignments provided by God. God would not give you someone that will push you away from him. A soul mate is not based on outer appearance (flesh); they look at your soul. Attraction must be there, but you do not need to compare yourself to other people because beauty is in the eyes of the beholder.

One thing I have learned about love is that there is a formula to falling in love. It requires attraction, vulnerability, and quality time (memories and experiences together). You can fall in love with anyone with this equation. When dating, instead of gathering information to see if this person is a suitable life partner (spouse), we first focus on creating connection and chemistry (emotional/ physical attachment). This tends to mess with our judgment. We find out that this person is not a suitable life partner, but we have invested so much time and fallen in love that we stay because of the attachment. Therefore, we must stop dating without purpose.

When you date with a purpose, it is intentional, and you treat it like an employer would treat a job interview and the 90-day probation period. A date does not mean they are qualified; it means they met the initial appearance test of attractiveness. This would be equivalent to an employer giving you an interview based on your resume. A beautiful/ experienced resume can still lead to a poor interview and unhired status. Even with the higher-level positions, you must do a series of interviews before consideration and then at least a standard 90-day probationary period to truly prove you are who you proclaim. Why does that not happen in dating? After a few dates, we have hired the person to enter a connection (physical or emotional) with us, and we are not taking precautions with our hearts. We are not properly guarding our hearts, and then when it is broken, we just put up a wall so no one can get in. I remember the early 2000s when the question was, do you wait 90 days to have sex, or would having sex right away affect the relationship? The answer is sex before marriage affects your judgment in selecting a suitable life partner. I say it from experience and never out of judgment for those who still believe in that process. I love all God's children equally. But I told myself I am done living like this, so I only engage in intentional dating. When I meet someone, I allow the following 7 questions or topics to guide the conversation:

1. I am abstinent, what is your status?
2. I am looking for a man of God.

3. What do you do for your community (I love outreach and do not plan to stay home often)?
4. How is your relationship with God?
5. How is your prayer life?
6. What are your purpose and your gifts from God?
7. Are you aware of your family's generational curses?

You never know who you are marrying when you choose not to include God in your relationship decisions. If you choose to include God in your decision-making process, God knows who you are marrying better than you ever could. So, if you consult with him on the true matters of your significant other's heart and he tells you not to marry that person, DO NOT try to petition him. Instead, thank him for giving you foresight and protecting you from whatever that person may do in the future. We tend to make decisions based on the now or the past. Since God is all-knowing, God makes decisions based on our futures. The devil does not just tempt your relationships when you are dating. When you get married, the devil sits there and attempts to destroy your marriage by finding the little things that we leave unresolved in ourselves. He tries to amplify them so that we would want to leave the marriage because we think that they are damaged or are not who we initially married. Turns out, we married the same person; they just had issues that they left dormant and are now resurfacing. When you marry someone, it is not because of who they currently are; it is a decision to say that this person is worth fighting for and overcoming obstacles, in any season, in our lives together. This means whatever comes your way, you fight it together and not singularly.

When God recommends a suitable partner for you, this person meets your soul needs (soul mate). It does not mean that this person may not have a generational curse that has not yet been broken, but God understood and knew what you could handle. He would not give you a trial that you could not triumph over with his help. Trust the process, trust God's will for you and have faith that he will help you to help your spouse beat that generational curse and vice versa. God does not pick your partner; he gives you suitable soul mate prospects, and you decide which one. You should base it on what you value in a partner and your purpose. For me, hygiene is everything, so it is a deal-breaker. If God feels one of the prospects would give you the best outcome (more spiritual growth, challenges you to evolve and support all God's assignments and amplifies them), God will say "they are the one" like any father would. Maybe it is just a simple issue that your spouse may struggle with. God knows you can be the one to be his image bearer in your marriage that will help your spouse overcome their issues. He knows you can make your marriage prosper, regardless of adversity, so your marriage can now be an example for the rest of the world. It will be a testimony that God is real, and so it is God's love. To be an image-bearer of God, understanding the New Testament and how Jesus showed love, mercy, and gave forgiveness, grace, and peace to everyone. This is what he wants to show the lost souls in the world to let them know that there is a place called Home for them in him.

There is a difference between God telling us that this person is the one for us and us just having a feeling because everything seems good and promising. Some people would stay together for years before they get married because they think they need to know the person very well before marriage. However, you can be with someone for 10 years and finally get married and then turn around and get divorced. As we only can see the past and present, we ALONE cannot determine our future, including our spouse's character. Some people fail to realize that a Divine Union is not the same as a society's depiction of marriage. When people get into a marriage based on society's standards, they must know the person well enough to decide. They do not consider that it is limited because you can only know what the person tells you. Isn't that a scary thought? That is probably what causes people to wait so long. Fortunately for us, God does not give us a spirit of fear but of power, love, and SOUND mind, 2 Timothy 1:7. Learn to trust that God knows what is best for you and understand that he has your best interest at heart. He knows the number of hairs on your head, and he knows you by name because he is your father, and he loves you. A divine union by God is when God tells you of the person that he recommends for you to marry because he deems that individual worthy of his child. Of course, you have the choice to pursue the marriage that God has ordained for you. If you do, his anointing is over your marriage which means it can outlast the test of times.

I chose the word "can" because it is a choice you must make, intentionally, every day to seek unity, love, and give grace, and forgiveness. A love that mirrors God's love for the church is key. Sometimes we assume that it is God's doing because it feels or seems right. This person may have met the requirements that we have placed over the years, after dating or based on what society has shown us. As Pastor Mike Todd says, "RIP THE LIST!" Unfortunately, that is not enough to help us determine if a person is meant for you or if they are of God's will for your life. You must seek God on the matters of this to truly be of his will for your life. Even with spiritual maturity, we may decipher if something is true of God or if something is truly what we need. We should still consult God for confirmation because the devil sends counterfeits.

Relationships take patience and consistent acts of selflessness. Your husband must learn how to lead you. Husbands may lead and make sound decisions, but there is a partnership that requires collaboration. He must learn how to lead his wife and understand her processes, needs, and take the time to love her the way she needs to be loved. Look into Gary Chapman's book called Love Languages. Women must give their husbands room for error and help guide them towards what they need from them. This takes away the pressure of performance and just leaves the important parts about building intimacy through vulnerability. This would allow for more time for both partners to focus on pursuing purpose and less on offenses and unspoken expectations. This gives room for grace and mercy to be foundational traits in your marriage. At my current job, when our new CEO took office, she made it her point to meet with all department leaders. She wanted to understand their processes, their current challenges, and their expectations of her. This allows her to lead our organization properly. This is an example of what would transpire with you and your husband. You would get to know life together and build a foundation based on that. Making mistakes, forgiving each other, and learning from those mistakes is key. Marriage is a lifelong adventure, and no one will be perfect, but we are always progressing. Learn to enjoy the process and give grace, mercy, and forgiveness because they are a foundational part of marriage.

Proper Planning Prevents Poor Performance

In terms of my past relationships, if I discovered infidelity, I would always strategically plan my breakups and not operate off impulse/at the moment. The moment I find out bad news is not the time to confront or pursue someone because that can lead to an altercation or lead a less than the preferable outcome for me. So, I choose to internalize the issue and strategize a way to end the relationship after getting all my belongings from his possession, i.e. if he owes me money. I treat it as an employer would. They plan out the logistics of the termination before they terminate the employee. I also like to bring proof to justify why I am breaking up with them. If I had found out about infidelity while being near the person (from their mobile devices) or even away from the person I choose to internalize it.

I internalize my emotions inside, and throughout the day, I strategize the next step. By this time, I have come to terms that the relationship is over. During the logistical period, my main concern is how to secure my assets before breaking up and where I would live. I try to make the breakup as neutral and logistical as possible because I need them to understand that this relationship was not meant to be. If I am doing all I can for that relationship to work and that person still cheats or does wrong by me, I must let them go. I had my internal battles, and I was still working on my security and identity. I could not handle the stress of trust issues as well. I had to decide just to terminate the relationship because it is harder for me to remain in the girlfriend role while grieving the loss of trust and love in the relationship due to betrayal. Healing must occur within me, and I cannot properly heal while meeting the obligations assigned to that role. I would never grieve until after the breakup is officially over. At that time, I would cry out all my pain and tell God to take away the pain and the emotions. He then works with me through the process.

This explanation was an understanding of how I plan to bring similar concepts to my marriage if I ever caught my husband cheating. Pastor Dharius Daniels says to plan for the pain; not to anticipate the pain but to plan just in case this ever happens. If I found out my husband was cheating on me, I would make plans and provisions to confront him that same day. Before I do, I would need to meditate and seek God. As God told me, this is the man for me; God knows my husband's mind and heart, so God understands how I need to handle the situation. No one will ever know their spouse 100%, but God does so to decide based on what I am feeling, at the time, would not be beneficial for my marriage; especially if I plan to stay. To stay and just be miserable or unforgiving is like hell on Earth in a marriage. Reconciliation is REQUIRED if you plan to stay, not torment and condemnation. My plan is not to divide the assets after a betrayal in my marriage; it is to restore unity in the marriage. I would meditate on the word to gain understanding. If I find out about the infidelity while I am at work or doing something important, I will have to leave early. I would have to stop what I am doing because I treat this betrayal like a death in the family. It requires grieving. I would pursue my meditation with God because, at this point, I am grieving and will have to give the necessary time for the grieving process. We must grieve the loss of trust, love, and friendship. To keep me from leaving, I will need God's miraculous love and healing to repair my soul and heart. I believe anything loss God can restore. The journey from infidelity is tough and feels like you are grieving the loss of life.

After I meditate with God, I will then proceed to confront my spouse regarding the infidelity. After confronting my spouse, I must go through the healing process, and I will need adequate space to heal. I plan to seek God, meditate on God's word, resolve my healing with God and have God pour into me because mankind cannot heal mankind. When someone apologizes it serves as an acknowledgment that they hurt you and will be intentional about not making the same mistakes again. An apology is a form of respect but is not an invitation for healing. Healing comes through closure with God, not the person. Allow God to renew your mind about the experience and show you how he can use it to bless you or others in the end. Only God can heal mankind, so for me to go to my husband and expect him to say something that would justify or make me feel better would just be me disappointing myself. I know that I am not in a place to receive his apologies of any sort, so it would not make sense to pursue it. I believe that if someone is not ready to receive, they will not receive the revelation. To expect my husband to say something that could alter my feelings when I am still grieving would waste both of our time, and therefore, the spouse that cheated must constantly apologize and prove themselves. We are seeking healing and validation from a human when we should be going back to Christ for him to reestablish our identity, and our value and allow us to grieve properly.

When we seek validation from our spouse, we seek something that will not heal the pain or patch the wound. Instead of pursuing an apology tour, let us first go to God and seek healing. Do not continue to vent to your spouse because you want to see more remorse in them. As much as we think remorse would fill the void, it does not. The enemy's attack planted a seed in us that we must allow God to extract from the ROOT. We must understand that the attack was from the enemy operating in our spouse, so first, seek healing and regain an understanding of our identity in Christ so that we can prepare for battle. We must find the underlined issues that caused the infidelity, which was the enemy trying to attack your marriage. As God says in Ephesians 5, marriage is supposed to be an image-bearer of God's love for the church. We must understand that the devil is constantly attacking the church so that he will attack our marriage. When there are things in your marriage left in the dark due to shame, lack of intimacy, or communication, it gives the devil the advantage. If your spouse is struggling with pornography, addiction, or insecurity and is not vulnerable enough to share these shortcomings, it is dangerous. Things left in the dark allow the enemy to use our spouse for sin because it is now an internal battle, and the flesh is winning. We must build that level of intimacy with our spouse and be intentional about addressing any issues, as they arise, versus dealing with the aftermath. Not saying that this infidelity was our fault, but to understand that we must be vigilant because the enemy is always trying to attack us. With transparency, there will be no room for the enemy to plant any seeds within us that will cause us to fall to his temptations.

Ephesians 5:25 NLT: "For husbands, this means love your wives, just as Christ loved the church. He gave up his life for her."

Remember always to separate the human from the sin. It is the devil who took a jab at you, not your spouse. Of course, this is easier said than done, but if you plan for the pain, you will always have something to reference when you cannot think logically. When you have this reference in place, you would remember to take it to God FIRST as much as it hurts. He will know how to take care of a broken heart and repair it. He will tell you how you should handle your spouse. Nothing will be accomplished if you take matters into your own hands and then choose to consult with God after all the negative words and attacks were made in retaliation. Retaliation leaves scars as well, and that is what the devil wanted. Degrading someone and making them feel less than or bringing up old stuff are forms of toxic traits that can destroy any relationship. It does not heal a wound but instead creates another, and then we are shocked when the offender is no longer remorseful. We are all human, and we all have feelings. Even when we make mistakes, we still need to give grace as God gives it to us every time we have sinned against him.

Meanwhile, the devil is just laughing in the corner, watching the demise of your relationship, and planning his next attack on you or your child. Remember, he needs to plant wicked seeds in the children while you and your spouse are distracted fighting each other or divorce. I painted a real picture because we must see that the enemy only comes to kill, steal, and destroy, and that means BY ANY MEANS NECESSARY. He does not care for your political, professional, or spiritual position or your influence. He wants your life to be miserable if you follow God. Sadly, he does not have the authority to have his way, so he tricks us into causing our demise. Then for the non-believers: he is just waiting for them to die so he can claim their souls in Hell. When we do not plan for the pain, we will be fighting and not reconciling which will not lead to healing. We will not focus on purpose but be distracted. The devil needs us distracted so he can advance his agenda. If the goal is reconciliation, you must first go to God after the betrayal because you need to grieve what you have just experienced properly. You do not just automatically go back to work after a loved one has died. You go to God for healing and family/friends for support, and you then go to the funeral. You take some time to reflect, and once you have begun the healing process with God (ideally) or feel you can make logical decisions, you then return to work. Use that same logic with your marriage after infidelity or deep betrayal. You do not go back to work and be a spouse. You step back and just be a child of God and let him work on you and heal your broken heart.

Then God will help you forgive your spouse for allowing the enemy to use them. After healing, we should pursue our spouse's apologies and request full confession because there was an underlined issue, and if not resolved, the devil will use it again. Once the issue is revealed, we must allow God to work with our spouse to move forward; we fight all internal battles together. Some underlying issues from infidelity can be pornography or insecurity because the devil uses things as a gateway to utilize someone. As I spoke about sin in previous chapters, all these sins are gateways for the enemy to plant suggestions that discourage us, distract us, condemn us, and/or allow us to make poor decisions because of our flesh (urges for self-gratification). Our flesh will be more powerful than our spiritual (self-control). During sin, our spirit is non-operated. Our fleshly desires are being activated and enticed by the temptations of the devil, so if you do not get ahead of it, you can be a product of it (sin patterns), or you can make someone a victim of it (infidelity, betrayal, etc.).

From Paper to Process

I do believe betrayal (lies and infidelity) is redeemable through God and him alone. No one can determine your marriage's outcome besides you and God, so anytime you experience infidelity or any kind of betrayal, bring it to God first. See what he says for you to do. I recommend a fast so that you lessen your flesh and activate your spirit. Spend time in deep meditation with God and allow the grieving to begin. Your marriage reconciliation will be a testimony of God's love for the church. Your testimony can be the flame that ignites someone else's reconciliation of their marriage. Let us be that beacon of hope that someone who may have experienced what you experienced. They may want to repair their marriage and see the power of God through your marriage. You could be the couple that inspires non-believers to seek out God to save their marriage. It is not about how someone gets to God. It is about us blessing someone with the opportunity to experience God for themselves so that they can be saved and redeemed as rightful heirs to Christ. People may not understand that the devil lives to try to attack us, especially as Christ-followers. The devil attacks anyone who is a threat to him. For the Christ-followers that know their identity in Christ, they are a force to be reckoned with. The devil does not focus his attacks on the non-believers as much because all he must do is keep them entangled in sin patterns, and they will be their demise in the end. Even the Christians who have sinned patterns that they leave unresolved; this is a method that the devil uses to ensure that you do not find purpose in God and identity in Christ. Instead, you would be of this world and base yourself and your value on society's standards. The devil does not have to concern himself with people stuck in sin patterns because he knows it will keep us distracted as we lose sight of who we are in Christ and not pursue purpose in God's plan for humanity.

As believers, when our purpose is to do God's will and spread God's love on Earth, the devil tries to attack us, so we will not finish our mission. He sends offenses; he sends betrayals; he sends anger our way. Until we start to recognize his attacks, we will be left fighting battles that were already won and missing out on purpose. So, when the devil tries to attack you or even your marriage, do not get even, Level Up! If you want to truly upset the devil, save a soul, show acts of kindness, show God's love to humanity and combat darkness with light. We are the light of the world, and God needs us to shine bright. When you want to get back at the devil, do God's will, and you would be crushing his plans and reminding him how powerless he is. Therefore, we must plan for the pain of betrayal because arguing with our spouses or divorcing our spouses over an offense will only bring pain to ourselves and our spouses, and the devil gets the point. Ask God how to proceed because he knows what is best for his children. Just remember that with Faith comes obedience which leads to Miracles and Testimonies.

Recommendations

God is listening, and he sees what we go through. He makes it his point to make resources available in the form of sermons or literature. They can help us through singleness, dating, marriage, and even remarriage, so do not just sit stagnate due to ignorance. The listed individuals and organizations on my acknowledgment page are organizations and/or companies that poured into my understanding of God. Because my situation is not your situation, completely, I spoke on my revelations from the resources God provided me. If you ask God to lead you, then he will surround you with the right people and give you the same resources as he did for me. They talk heavenly about all types of relationships, marriage, and identity (self-awareness), so please seek the resources and allow God to pour into your situation. My only recommendation outside of literature is that if you meet someone with unresolved issues (damaged) and choose to date them, I do not recommend that. If you are dating them and you find out about those issues, I recommend downgrading that relationship to a friendship. Giving that person sex or a relationship and expecting them to change is not ideal. Do not give until the basic requirement has been met. We are not supposed to use sex or relationship to incentivize them to change. It must be of their own will for their lives, or they will relapse. When sex is removed, other forms of intimacy can heighten, just as we lose one of our five senses. It allows us to show love in a different way that encourages change.

10

LOVE CONQUERS ALL

In every relationship you have, you must have grace and mercy. Without those two things, we tend to become selfish and concerned with just our needs and what the person did to us. Instead, show humility and empathy because you cannot see the pressure the other person is under, and the other person cannot see the pain you are in. This is life whether it is with work, family, feelings, or friends. We should try to understand each other. Learn to think differently, perhaps more clearly, and communicate better. A little love and patience go a long way.

To truly succeed at "making it work" in your relationship, you must see your actions during a test. When during the hard times, if you choose to show love versus hate and grace or mercy over condemnation, then you are truly giving your all to making your relationship work. Everyone can "try to make it work" during the good times, but it is in the moments when your significant other or your friend gets on your nerves, that you show patience. When your significant other or friend is mad and begins to speak out of character (swearing and being rude), you do not match their energy. Choosing not to reciprocate the negative behavior they are displaying requires peace, love, and discipline (practice). Instead, advise them by saying, "We are not going to argue and be mean to each other because we love each other. Take some space and let us gather our thoughts so we can discuss this with love". Of course, this is easier said than done, but nothing worth it will come easy. The question is, how bad do you truly want to make it work? Never seek to argue, but have a productive discussion because when the intention is to improve a situation, it is handled with hope and positivity versus negativity. Arguments, especially while you are mad, only lead to destruction and pain. Trying to bring peace and unity when times are hard is how you rise above and win, so think of this the next time you tell yourself or others that you "tried to make it work."

Love heals all wounds; pride only brings doom.

I heard this story, and it was profound: A snake crawled over a sharp saw and was cut. In anger, the snake wrapped the saw with its thick body and proceeded to squeeze the life out of the saw. With each angry squeeze, it felt more pain but continued because it would not let the saw get away with the pain it caused it. The snake refusing to let go of the saw eventually died, not knowing the whole time he needed to let go of the initial pain and focus on its future and where it was going. Instead, the snake, unfortunately, lost its life and did not even see it coming. The moral of the story is to control your anger. Do not give people power over you. In any relationship, always keep a spirit of learning. Your spouse or friend is always evolving, and if they are following God, they are always in the season of transformation. So, do not be prideful and assume you know everything about your spouse or friend. Your faith is not in knowing everything about your spouse or friend. It is in knowing who God is and how he will always protect you. So, trust God always to have your best interest at heart and put your marriage and friendships in his hands. Maintain a posture of learning. Be at peace with being wrong sometimes. It is not about wrong or right but about always maintaining unity. Sometimes we fight for the need to be right and lose unity in the process, so is it worth it? Do not manifest the spirit of pride because that can be the destruction of your relationships. Remember, the 7 deadly sins are just that…deadly. They bring death to whatever they touch because they are gateway sins that can manifest into greater destruction. These are the plans of the enemy.

Learn to listen. Active listening is important, and the spirit of pride makes us focus on our response rather than listening to the person. Admitting when you do not know something or when you are wrong helps combat the prideful spirit. Apologize often. Not being willing to learn from someone because you think they are not knowledgeable enough to give you advice is a spirit of pride. We must remember that God will use anyone to advance his Divine agenda. God qualifies the call, so when you think that someone in sin cannot give you advice, that is wrong. Before I got saved, I was given wisdom as a gift from God, and I shared it with anyone willing to listen.

Giving your advice and seeing their potential can nurture their gifts from God and help them pursue a deeper connection with Christ. That was my story. At the start of 2020, I would have never thought I could be a coach or writer/author. I always thought I just was an "old soul" and that I was supposed to give my advice and wisdom to my friends or whoever wanted it. God surrounded me with like-minded Christ believers at my job. It took my coworkers to understand that my gift was more and should be spread to the world. So, here I am writing my story to you. Sometimes when people are stuck in their sin patterns, we do not need to judge them. Let us help motivate them to seek more out of life by seeing that their life has a purpose. Helping them to realize their gifts and let them know that God could help them cultivate their gifts to build wealth. This would motivate them to seek out God.

Once the interest is ignited, leave the rest to God. It is not our job to convert people to Christianity by force. It is our job to be image-bearers and to spread the word of the Lord. Like when you see ads on social media that tell you "My story on how I started making 6 figures a year", if we have a goal of living that kind of lifestyle, we will click the ads and learn more. It is the same thing with Christianity. We are supposed to live fruitful lives and be God's image-bearers of love, grace, mercy, forgiveness, peace, prosperity, etc. God will continue to pour the blessings over our lives to use as a beacon for his lost children. And with every testimony comes that spark of inspiration in someone, a non-believer or someone who struggles with a sin pattern, that would cause them to ask questions of how they can live a life as fruitful. Our job is to show them how life can be with God and remind them that the enemy is real. However, God gave us authority over him. We should teach them how to conquer spiritual warfare and build their faith to prosper in their spiritual journey with God.

Saved lives save lives!

God comes to let you know he loves you just the way you are regardless. As he sent his son to die for your sins, he knew that this life would be hard and that temptation can sometimes overpower us. All he wants to do is help us get better so that we can, in turn, help the next person through our testimony. He shows you what he plans for your life to maximize the life that you have regardless of what you went through. Then he surrounds you with people who constantly remind you of how great you are, and they help you be the best version of yourself so that you can get to where you need to be. Be a beacon of hope for someone else who went through something that you have conquered with God because they need the love of God over their lives. God wants to show you a better life for you, but he will not force it on you. You must want it for yourself because he gives us free will to do what we want. God is a gentleman. When we forget what God got us through, we tend to develop pride and judge others. We failed to realize that our testimony has a purpose because God uses it as a beacon for his lost children. So, always remember what God has brought you through and be intentional with your day because you never know when someone needs that testimony to transform their life. Saved lives save lives.

As it says in James 4 explains that we must not seek things of fleshly desires because they will not follow us to the afterlife, nor will they fill the fulfillment void in our life.

James 4: 1-4 NIV: "What causes fights and quarrels among you? Do not they come from your desires that battle within you? You desire but do not have, so you kill. You covet, but you cannot get what you want, so you quarrel and fight. You do not have because you do not ask God. When you ask, you do not receive, because you ask with wrong motives, that you may spend what you get on your pleasures. You, adulterous people, do not you know that friendship with the world means enmity against God? Therefore, anyone who chooses to be a friend of the world becomes an enemy of God."

Self-gratifications will leave you on a consistent journey that will have you thinking life is meaningless. This path may bring quick spurts of happiness, but it is not fulfilling. God knows what you need, and he will provide for your needs. We sometimes fear that he cannot meet our needs because his needs are different from ours. Since we view things from a past and present perspective, it can cloud our minds to think God does not know the future. As God tells us to plan for today and leave tomorrow for him, that kind of faith we all have a goal of one day obtaining. However, being raised in today's society, we will need many reprogramming and trust exercises to get there. He understands our current situation, and he would not tell us to trust him if he did not plan to secure us where we go. Instead of thinking about the next step, just trust him to lead you to that next step. These trust exercises help grow our faith and give us a testimony to inspire the next person to seek and trust in God. Everything God does for us is to allow His will to be done and for God's glory. The lost will find their way back to their father through us as believers. He uses us (saved people of God) as a beacon for his lost children because as they seek him, they need us, as his image-bearers, to help them understand who he is and how he loves. As the devil tries so hard to tarnish the name of the Lord, we must help restore and represent God to the lost and found.

Jeremiah 31:3 NIV: "Where the Lord appears to us saying I have loved you with an everlasting love, I have drawn you with unfailing kindness."

11

BLAME BAD DOCTRINE, NOT GOD.

Just because someone has a church title, speaks in tongues, can quote scripture, etc., does not mean that they have God. You must use discernment to determine if someone has the "Spirit" by the fruit they bear and their fruit alone. Suppose someone is pastoring a church that is packed out every Sunday; that does not matter. None of this is expected to suggest to you that they know God. For us to survive the tsunami of darkness that is reaching our world, it will take real force. You can let what harmed you tear you apart, or you can see it as an opportunity to look at life differently in a whole new light. Love cast out fear, and hate, and exposes the plans of the enemy. For where there is fear, there is torment. Faith and God's perfect love cast out all fear. We cannot do anything in God without God's love. We cannot move, minister, prophesy or use his authority without Him. The enemy tries to choke out the love in us because he knows we will need God's love to do his work. Guard your heart, and do not seek out things that will cause you pain. Pray for the gift of discernment, love, and other fruits of the spirit like forgiveness. Faith will open the door, but love takes us on and keeps us there in his presence.

Colossians 2:22-23 NKJV: "*Which all concern things which perish with the using— according to the commandments and doctrines of men? These things indeed have an appearance of wisdom in self-imposed religion, false humility, and neglect of the body, but are of no value against the indulgence of the flesh.*"

I have been in church all my life. I was raised around God and Christianity, but 2019 is when I understood God. I had to stop compartmentalizing God and assuming that his role in my life was only in certain aspects of my life. 2019 helped me understand that he is the almighty God and that condemnation is not his nature. There is no limit to what I can achieve with him on my side because he is my Father, and I am a Vine from his fruitful Branch. Unfortunately, with some churches, we can experience instances of very judgmental individuals. They shame teenage mothers and shame people who cannot get released from their sin patterns. They make you believe that you are the problem. They are the problem because they failed to understand that church is a hospital for God's children. It is not a popularity contest or a place where you boast of your ability to avoid sin. All the knowledge I have explained in this book was knowledge I learned the hard way or by God. Some churches focus more on routine than relationship building with Christ. They lived on the foundation of the Old Testament and built their foundation on performance. They forget that Jesus died so that we no longer had to earn God's grace but that through repentance, it was given.

Colossians 2:8-10 MSG: "*Watch out for people who try to dazzle you with big words and intellectual double-talk. They want to drag you off into endless arguments that never amount to anything. They spread their ideas through the empty traditions of human beings and the empty superstitions of spirit beings. But that is not the way of Christ. Everything of God gets expressed in him, so you can see and hear him clearly. You do not need a telescope, a microscope, or a horoscope to realize the fullness of Christ and the emptiness of the universe without him. When you come to him, that fullness comes together for you, too. His power extends over everything."*

It is unfortunate when bad doctrine is something that keeps people away from God. It is the devil's attack on the Church. When a church is operating like a business or a club and not for God's will it is of bad doctrine. The Bible is a history book and a love letter that God felt could show man the history of his love for us. From the creation of man, out of his love and image, to the fall of Man by sin. Then everyone's individual encounter with God throughout the Old Testament. Then the New testament is where God sent his only begotten son to die for our sins. This act of true love allowed us to be restored to God and not fall under the feet of the devil. The Bible tells us of everyone's encounter with the Trinity (God, Jesus, and Holy Spirit). You must learn from each encounter that God just wanted his children, whom he loves with all his heart, to love and honor him back. The New Testament explained how we no longer were judged by our standards but by the grace of Jesus, and no one can undo what is ordained.

Do not allow society's decision to condemn one another to affect your relationship with God. When we die, we will be judged based on ourselves, not on someone else. So, for those who do not believe because of bad doctrine, do not let other people rob you of your chance at eternity and happiness. The Bible is of stories by people who are no longer alive, which means it is based on our interpretation. This can be limited based on our limited perspectives and worldviews. You could read the same verse at 10 years old and again at 27 years old and get a different understanding because of your experiences. However, when you seek out God and ask him to provide you with wisdom, he will start to give you clarification. He will even surround you with people that will bring that understanding to you because he wants the chance to explain his love for you. God is an awesome father. He has no problem helping you understand what was meant for you to understand from the story. Reading the Bible to understand it and reading the Bible just to read does impact our understanding of God. If you receive bad doctrine growing up or went to multiple churches and received bad doctrine, that does not change who God is. Even good people can give me bad information. We must have forgiveness in our hearts. When we have a bad car buying experience at a dealership, we do not just never buy a car again. We find a different car dealership and purchase the vehicle. It is the same with the Church. You must establish boundaries and be intentional. As churches are organizations, review their mission and visions to see if they stand on a faulty foundation. We are the light in this world, so do not lose your light for anyone. Whether it is darkness operating in a Church or a misunderstanding, it is our job to reveal the errors of their ways and warn others of them. In 2021, let us not think about victimizing ourselves anymore. Instead, we need to try to pursue God through him and not through man. He will surround you with the right people, and you do not have to worry about how or who; that is what faith is for. Let God know that you are willing to give him a fair chance with your heart; you will not be disappointed. You must also pray for the gift of discernment so that God can let you see who is not teaching his word properly.

James 1:5 NIV: "If any of you lacks wisdom, you should ask God, who gives generously to all without finding fault, and it will be given to you."

From Paper to Process

Bad doctrine can be easily overlooked but is also very easy to spot. Some of the traits you would find in a church with a bad doctrine are Churches that condemn you for not tithing. Churches that follow Old fashion worldviews based on the Old Testament that stated that women should not lead and that women are supposed to be submitted to men versus just their husbands. A church that tells you what to wear. A church that tells you not to wear jewelry because it is a form of idolatry, but the pastor's face or church symbol is plastered on everything. The Church condemns and shames you for your sin and does not focus on helping you overcome sin patterns. Churches were gossiping overlooked and not addressed. When the pastor seems more like a dictator and not a leader who hears his people. I am sorry but RUN if this is your Church. The church does not define your spirituality, your relationship with God does. It takes intentionality to build that with him.

Colossians 2:7-8,22-23 NLT: "Let your roots grow down into him, and let your lives be built on him. Then your faith will grow strong in the truth you were taught, and you will overflow with thankfulness. Do not let anyone capture you with empty philosophies and high-sounding nonsense that come from human thinking and the spiritual powers of this world rather than from Christ. Such rules are mere human teachings about things that deteriorate as we use them. These rules may seem wise because they require strong devotion, pious self-denial, and severe bodily discipline. But they provide no help in conquering a person's evil desires."

12

GOD'S HEALING POWER

You can let what harmed you tear you apart, or you can see it as an opportunity to look at life in a whole new light. Sometimes the devil's plot is not always to kill but to take away something from us that makes us unable to fulfill our purpose. Our perception of things changes. God must go through a series of seasons with us, so we experience a mindset adjustment. He starts by bringing us back to the basics so that he can renew our minds to align with his word. As hard as that season is, it is necessary for the purpose we are called to fulfill. He must uproot the planted seeds of the enemy and establish our true identities in Christ.

Like when Moses delivered the Israelites from slavery and brought them to the wilderness. God brought the Israelites to the wilderness and only fed them manna to allow for his process of reconstruction to begin. They had to understand who God was to them. God wanted to be viewed as their provider and the one who redeemed them from slavery. He also wanted to give them identity and teach them faith before he can provide the purpose. So, it is not because God does not love us that we are going through a shift. The process is necessary to prevent bad traits from hindering our purpose. The mindset shift process requires us to be broken and remove all our negative perceptions of him and ourselves. In this process, we understand God, and our identities in him, and let go of friends who do not bear fruit in our lives. You can also lose opportunities that would distract you from your purpose. God needs you to focus on what he is trying to do for you, and distractions only delay destiny. We must take away that fear of missing out because God will restore and provide all that was lost tenfold. God can accelerate your dreams and qualify you for things people did not think you were qualified for. He takes the nobodies and turns them into some bodies. You will not be missing out on anything when you follow God's process because he created heaven and the Earth and all its inhabitants. Obedience and faith in God, during the process, will help to propel you into purpose the right way.

Victims need rehabilitation to help them remember who they are. They need to understand that they did not deserve that pain. They have a choice to change their future. They have a voice, and they must forgive to remove the mental bondage from their life. Like when God took the Israelites to the wilderness to help them unlearn the slavery mindset. He needed them to become warriors so that they can claim the promised land. God provided for them and wanted to teach them faith and obedience. Their inability to adapt kept them stagnant in their lives.

Healing from past traumas takes strength and perseverance. You must be intentional because the enemy will try to discourage your progression. To experience true healing requires forgiveness. If you get to a place of forgiveness, the enemy cannot keep you bound and distract you from purpose. Without proper healing, relapse can occur during the process of recovery. Some people may not be able to assist with your recovery process because they have suppressed those issues. It can feel counterproductive when you attempt to resolve your past issues with someone who is not ready to confront their issues. You are requesting someone to relive those memories with you, and it is not fair to them. Seek out help from a professional because your story is important, and there is someone ready to listen. Do not feel overwhelmed or discouraged. You must understand that not everybody can live in their truth yet. Everybody is not ready for their breakthrough. Some tend to suppress their emotions and their past, which can manifest into poor choices and behaviors.

There are different levels of scars, and each one requires God's power of healing. Mankind cannot heal mankind; Only God can. Mankind can help someone receive a revelation from God, but that is through the Holy Spirit. We must allow time with God for him to heal our hearts of pain. When the devil comes to steal, kill, and destroy, his goal is to cut us so deep that the scar never heals. Then he attempts to rip off the bandage in your mind to cause you to seek relief with drugs, alcohol, sex, etc. We must identify the pattern he keeps us in when we do not heal from betrayals, abuse, etc. You must grasp the understanding that holding on to pain only keeps you bound and unable to love properly. You miss out on the blessings of God because you hold on to the pain of the enemy's attacks. The devil's attacks are always when you least expect them because they will leave the biggest scar. There is a powerful healing that can take place that will leave you with peace, but it requires God. We are responsible for our healing. We must seek it by any means because to suffer alone is not the end of your story. You are more than a conqueror, and God will get you through the healing.

When we need healing from losing a loved one, we must remember the good memories. Thank God for the memories we had with that individual. We must not be sad because they are at peace. We must understand that this world is not forever and that we all have an end date. We must love everyone like it is our last day on Earth because tomorrow is not promised but today is a blessing from God. If we did not make amends with the loved one who died, do not live with regret. Show your appreciation for the loved ones who are still here. Forgive and ask God for healing. Allow God to uproot the wall of offenses in your heart so that you can love wholeheartedly again.

Receive deliverance from your pain so that God could use you to teach others how to do the same. You will also be an example for your relatives to seek help with their issues. If your family is singling you out, it is normal when your path is different from theirs. You will be the one to break the generational curses, and you will be healed and ready for the next chapter of your life. Be the image-bearer of God, and he will work on your family. Continue to pray for them and leave it in God's hands. You must seek out people that God will surround you with to help you on your journey towards deliverance. It may not be the same people who experienced the trauma with you because everyone has their way of coping with it. God always surrounds you with the right group of people who will help uplift you and help you pray in times of weariness. These individuals have already overcome their issues and can now be your accountability partner. They are also a living testimony that healing is attainable. As we all know, the research and literature available today were not available during our parent's generation. When God has blessed you with wisdom, you must share it and forgive those who do not know. Be an example of how literature has renewed your life. Others will see your transformation and be motivated to pursue their healing. Teach others how to obtain deliverance and allow your testimony to be someone's hope.

From Paper to Process

The healing process is different for everyone. During my process of healing, God revealed to me the open wounds I did not properly treat. I created a spiritual bucket list that included different tasks like forgiving someone who hurt me and apologizing to someone I hurt. After I completed the task, I wrote down a list of all who have hurt me in the past. I wanted to understand what was keeping me held bound. With every person or instance, I brought it to God to seek healing. After reading Soul Care, I tried to imagine how God was there for me through it all. I also saw how the devil used that person and me to act out of character.

Anger may seem small, but it can manifest in different forms of abuse and betrayal. Understanding what happened and separating the human from the sin was the key to my forgiveness. Not everyone can love me, but I allowed everyone into my vulnerable space. I began to establish boundaries and increased my discernment through the word of God. I used his word to reevaluate the company I kept. God may use others to help you gain a deeper understanding of his work. Ultimately, your revelation itself is a blessing from the Holy Spirit. It is best to seek out God for understanding so that he can help heal you. Spend time in meditation so that he can restore you and allow you to grieve the heartaches. He will teach you that everyone makes mistakes, even you. He covered them all with grace and forgiveness. The enemy tries to use the people we love to hurt us, and we must get to the root of the problems and begin to identify his attacks on our lives.

CONCLUSION

If you would like to give yourself to Christ today, it is very easy, just speak these words below and know that Heaven is celebrating your salvation today, your true Father is Proud of you:

Romans 10:9-10: NIV *"If you declare with your mouth, Jesus is Lord, and believe in your heart that God raised him from the dead, you will be saved. For it is with your heart that you believe and are justified, and it is with your mouth that you profess your faith and are saved."*

www.ingramcontent.com/pod-product-compliance
Lightning Source LLC
Chambersburg PA
CBHW071406290426
44108CB00014B/1706